St
S
Hosannas,
& Songs

A Snapshot of Anglican Issues and Visions in Canada

Commissioned by the General Synod
of the Anglican Church of Canada

Sally Edmonds Preiner

ABC Publishing
ANGLICAN BOOK CENTRE
TORONTO ■ CANADA

To Bill,
and to our sons and daughters,
and to Bernard Erling,
who taught me how to say grace.

2002
Anglican Book Centre
600 Jarvis Street
Toronto, Ontario
Canada M4Y 2J6

National Library of Canada Cataloguing in Publication

Preiner, Sally Edmonds
Stained glass, sweet grass, hosannas, and songs : a snapshot of Anglican issues and visions in Canada : a study commissioned by the General Synod of the Anglican Church of Canada / Sally Edmonds Preiner.

ISBN 1-55126-386-6

1. Anglican Church of Canada. I. Anglican Church of Canada. General Synod.

BX5614.P73 2002 283'.71 C2002-904473-1

Printed in Canada

CONTENTS

FOREWORD

General Synod 2001 in Waterloo called for an "Intentional Listening" process leading up to its meeting in 2004. Part of the response to that request is found in these pages, a report from Environics on a number of regional "focus groups" carried out on behalf of General Synod.

These gatherings took place in a variety of regions, and included sessions with young people in Huron Diocese and with the Anglican Council of Indigenous Peoples in Edmonton. The report provides a snapshot of the Church from a particular angle at a particular time. While not exhaustive, it is substantial, and I believe it is rich with the insights of those who participated.

The questions posed might be questions you would like to use in your congregation or other ministry setting. If you do, no doubt you will find some responses that echo those in this report, and others that are quite different. While this report will be part of preparing for a review of the General Synod strategic plan in 2004, the Church in all its manifestations — local, diocesan, and regional — can benefit from seeking out the insights of its members.

This report, and the focus groups it describes, are the first of three phases: researching and interviewing; consolidating and proposing; and planning. It has been prepared for Anglicans, but others are invited to use it, learn from it, and comment on it. I hope that by making public this first phase of a strategic planning process, the Church will benefit and the General Synod will become more visible to the Church and to Canadians in general.

There is little doubt that the Anglican Church, both in its own right and as part of the fabric of Canadian society, faces significant challenges. By understanding our members and listening to other voices in our context, I trust we will strengthen our capacity to share in God's mission of wholeness and hope.

Yours faithfully,

Michael G. Peers
Archbishop and Primate
July 2002

ACKNOWLEDGEMENTS

Thank you to those in the Anglican Church of Canada who worked with us and supported us in our thoughts and efforts: Archbishop Michael Peers (Primate); Archdeacon Jim Boyles (General Secretary); Margaret Shawyer; Esther Wesley; Verna Firth; Todd Russell; and Marion Jenkins.

A special thanks to those who helped to organize our meetings and discussion sessions, drove us to our destinations through winter storms, and made wonderful snacks and great coffee in the Anglican tradition: Archdeacon Neil Kellett, Province of Canada; Archdeacon Colin Johnson, Province of Ontario; Archdeacon Derek Hoskin, Province of Rupert's Land; and Ms. Sally Clinton and Ms. Rayleen Nash, Province of British Columbia and Yukon.

As well, thank you to all staff at Environics Research Group in Toronto who helped to make this project a success, and particular thanks to Jane Armstrong for identifying the opportunity and to Kevin Shanahan for his generous intellectual sharing. Thanks for efforts above and beyond the call of duty to the production team: Alison Gorbould; Cathy McKim; Karen Hume; Sandra Sarner; and Steve Otto. A special and heartfelt thanks to Morgan MacLeod, who took on the role of "managing editor" and "project mother." I am deeply grateful for her help and support.

And thank you to all of those who participated in the discussion groups and workshops, and to the Anglican Foundation of Canada for its financial support.

Sally Edmonds Preiner
September 2002
Toronto, Canada

INTRODUCTION

In the spring of 2002, Environics Research Group was engaged by the Anglican Church of Canada to conduct qualitative research as part of an "intentional listening" process. The participants in this phase of intentional listening were drawn from each of the four ecclesiastical provinces, and included laity and clergy from across Canada. This report, the result of that work, is a "snapshot" of the Anglican Church of Canada at this time in its history.

The research approaches used in the processes of listening and learning that resulted in this report place considerable importance on context. People do not form ideas or opinions in isolation. Part of the quest to fully understand the perspectives of others is to consider their context and how it informs, and is influenced by, their thoughts and feelings. The people who were a part of this research process celebrate their faith in a church that is not static but dynamic, not isolated but connected to the changes and events of the world, and practise their faith in a world that presents them with issues of global, national, and local concern. Events both within and outside the Church are a part of the context in which their visions and issues must be placed.

In turn, this research itself has a context: the needs and goals of the Anglican Church of Canada that led to the commissioning of this report, the intended purposes of the research, and the choices made in designing and conducting it.

The following material is offered to the reader as part of the context, both of this report and of the people whose words and thoughts it seeks to reflect.[1]

THE ANGLICAN CHURCH IN CANADA

In 1893, representatives of the dioceses and ecclesiastical provinces of the Church of England in Canada came together in Winnipeg and set

---

1 We would like to acknowledge the invaluable assistance and support of the Anglican Church of Canada in providing the source materials that formed the basis of much of the contextual and background information presented here.

out to unify the Anglican Church in this country. Today, in Canada, more than 700,000 communicants of the Anglican Church of Canada worship in parishes from Vancouver Island to St. John's, Newfoundland, and from the country's southernmost point to the Arctic Circle. The Anglican Church of Canada supports churches in large urban areas, small rural villages, and in remote northern regions.

The Anglican Church of Canada is part of the worldwide Anglican Communion, the worldwide network of Anglican Christians. While the Church is known as the Anglican Church, the Church of England, or the Episcopal Church, depending on the region, all Anglican Christians are part of the wider Anglican family, unified under the leadership of the Archbishop of Canterbury in England.

The Anglican Church comprises lay persons, deacons, priests, and bishops. Deacons serve as a bridge between church and community, helping to interpret the needs and concerns of society to church leaders, and helping to support and nurture church members. The priest serves as a pastor and teacher to members of the Church, is responsible for worship, preaches, and supports members of the congregation as they reach out into their community. In the Anglican Church of Canada, both women and men are eligible for ordination. Bishops are elected by priests and lay people. They provide leadership and care for groups of congregations (a diocese), and serve as a link with the mission and ministry of the national and international Churches and with other faith traditions.

The Anglican Church is divided into regional groupings called "dioceses." Each diocese has its own bishop (or bishops), who have the overall responsibility for the spiritual well-being and administration of the churches within the area. Dioceses are grouped into larger administrative regions called ecclesiastical provinces. The Most Rev. Michael Peers is the head (called the Primate) of the national Church.

Every three years, approximately 300 representatives from dioceses across the country gather together at a meeting called the General Synod (synod means "the common road" or "the road together") to make decisions about the national work of the Church. The General Synod is the Church's national body. It was created in 1893 in order to carry out certain functions on a national basis. Chief among these are mission in Canada and mission overseas. Mission involves, according to the Anglican Church, "spreading the good news of God's love through Jesus Christ, by word and deed." Missionaries were the primary agents of mission throughout most of the 19th century and the earlier part of the 20th century. In recent times, both overseas and at home, mission has been characterized by working in partnership with the local community and responding to its expressed needs.

Between synods, a group called the Council of General Synod is authorized to make decisions on behalf of the wider Church. Other counsel or advice is given by the House of Bishops — a gathering of bishops and archbishops from across Canada who meet regularly to consult with each other on spiritual, moral, and leadership issues.

THE 1995 STRATEGIC PLAN

Since 1893, there have been periodic reviews to renew and reaffirm the mandate of the General Synod. In 1967–68, Price Waterhouse & Company was engaged to propose a restructuring of the General Synod. The report, accepted by General Synod 1969 and revised from time to time over the years, shaped the work of the Anglican Church of Canada until the early 1990s.

In 1992, the General Synod directed the National Executive Council to undertake a strategic planning process in consultation with all dioceses and provinces to direct the work of the General Synod and the National Office between 1995 and 2004. The result of the planning process — *Preparing the Way: A Strategic Plan for the Work of The Anglican Church of Canada 1995–2004* — was approved by General Synod 1995, and revised by General Synod 2001 to include healing and reconciliation with Indigenous peoples as a priority.[2]

In preparation for a review of the Strategic Plan in 2004, General Synod 2001 directed the Council of General Synod "to initiate and oversee a process of intentional listening to the church in the dioceses and parishes regarding the future life and work of the Anglican Church of Canada, with ongoing monitoring during the next triennium, and recommendation for future planning to come to General Synod 2004." The Council of General Synod approved a three-part review process: research and interviewing; consolidating and proposing; and planning. As part of the research and interviewing aspect of the review process, Environics Research Group was commissioned to conduct research in two phases: a qualitative research process (focus group workshops and discussion groups) and quantitative research (surveys).

---

2 For a detailed summary of the 1995 Strategic Plan, please consult Appendix C.

THE RESEARCH: INTENTIONAL LISTENING

The intentional listening process, of which this qualitative research is one part, will include, over time, both qualitative and quantitative survey research, as well as formal meetings, informal conversations, and both formal and informal dialogue. This report is the outcome of the first, qualitative, phase of research.

Intentional listening is a commitment to try to understand as fully as possible the range of context from the perspective of various stakeholders. It is a consciously disciplined attempt to ensure that the issues of importance to the speaker are not filtered too heavily through the experience and expectations of the listener.

Intentionally listening to the stories, the expression of feelings about issues and concerns, and the sharing of experiences of members of the broader community provides a meaningful and powerful tool for those charged with determining strategic direction.

The intent of this qualitative phase of the intentional listening process was to ensure that the voice, perspective, and context of Anglicans across Canada be heard and then respectfully shared with others in the Anglican community.

The results of this research are just a beginning. The survey work that follows will provide an understanding of the weight that each of these issues and ideas carries within the population of the Anglican Church across Canada. The other meetings, discussions, and dialogue will provide opportunities for sharing ideas, concerns, and vision. When completed, this intentional listening process will provide tools that can be used in determining the future strategic direction of the Church.

THE CONTEXT: A SNAPSHOT OF THE TIME

To fully understand this report, it must be placed in the context of its time. In keeping with the focus within the Anglican Church of Canada on mission and on partnership, the concerns of the people of the Church are not separate from the concerns of the world at large, though some concerns may impact differently upon people of faith.

In addition to the broader context — the political, social, and economic concerns of the people whose views are expressed in this report — the findings must also be placed within the context of the key concerns facing the Church itself: matters of faith, doctrine, liturgy, stewardship, and the relationships of the Church to the people who comprise it, the people it serves, and the people it has affected.

In conducting the workshops and discussion groups that form the basis of this report, participants were encouraged to consider both these contexts. They were asked about their concerns, about signs of enthusiasm and excitement, of decay and despair, of hope and vision — both within and outside of the Church. The Church context, for the purpose of this research, included the local church community, the parish and diocese, and the national and worldwide Anglican Churches. We defined the broader context both in terms of the secular community and in terms of other faith communities.

The secular context in which this report must be placed encompasses a vast range of concerns. The workshops and discussion groups were conducted in the spring of 2002, and global issues on the minds of Anglicans in Canada at that time included

- Terrorism and the attack on the World Trade Center and the Pentagon in the United States
- Escalation of military interventions and the use of force to resolve national and international conflict, in the name of the "war on terrorism," in Afghanistan, Israel, and the Philippines, and threats of military intervention against other nations such as Iraq
- Violence and civil war in countries as widespread as Columbia, Mexico, India, and Sudan
- Threat of war between Pakistan and India over the Kashmir
- Scandals on Wall Street over fraudulent accounting practices of companies such as Enron
- Major economic crisis in Argentina as a result of fiscal policies imposed by the IMF
- Attempted coup d'état in Venezuela, with suspected US involvement
- Ongoing protests against globalization and the exploitation of developing nations
- Drought and famine in Southern Africa
- Floods and other natural disasters around the globe
- Disease pandemics in many places in the world: HIV/AIDS, tuberculosis
- Increasing evidence of the effects of global warming on the environment
- Widespread adoption of biotechnology and bioengineering in agriculture and other areas
- Reproductive engineering: the production of test-tube babies in Nepal, the debate on human cloning
- Scandals in the Roman Catholic Church in the US over the covering-up of sexual abuse by priests

- Preparations for World Youth Day, a coming together of Roman Catholic Youth planned for the summer of 2002

The Church context in which this report must be placed is, at the core, a context of faith, and how faith is to be expressed in worship and lived in the world. At the time that this "snapshot" of the Church was taken, issues of concern within the Church itself included litigation arising from the role of the Anglican Church in residential schools, debate over the Church's position on homosexuality, same-sex unions, and the role of gays and lesbians within the Church, consideration of the ways that the Church has adapted to changing liturgical needs, and issues of diversity in culture and styles of worship in different congregations. As well, Anglicans in British Columbia were concerned over a referendum on principles to be adopted in treaty negotiations between the BC government and the province's First Nations, and the Church's response to the referendum. To facilitate the reader's understanding of the context in which these sessions were held, some background into these issues is presented here. Further information on these topics may be found in the Appendices.

Residential Schools

Before Confederation and through the first half of the 20th century, the policy of the Government of Canada toward the First Nations was assimilation. It was thought that the quickest route to "civilizing" and "converting" the Indigenous population was to forcibly remove children from their homes and communities, and place them in residential schools. There was considerable variation in how the schools operated but, in many cases, the children were forbidden to speak their mother tongues, their cultures were condemned as barbaric and their spirituality as heathen. By the end of the 19th century, a relationship had developed between the government and the churches, with the government establishing policy and providing most of the funds, and the churches operating the schools on behalf of the government.

Between 1820 and 1969, the Anglican Church administered 26 Indian residential schools. By 1969, after taking a hard look at its relationship with Indigenous peoples, the Church withdrew from the residential schools project and committed itself to building more just relationships with its Indigenous members, as well as advocating on behalf of the Indigenous population at large.

Most of the people involved in the schools were well-motivated by the standards of their day, even though they were participants in an abusive system. Some, according to the recollections of former students, were good people working within an oppressive system. Some were predators who abused the children physically or sexually. Most of the former students of the schools recall their experiences with pain and anger. Some recall their experiences positively. Many view with contempt the Church and government that tried to eradicate their culture. Others retain a powerful Christian faith (often combined with Indigenous tradition) and work within the Church on behalf of justice for all native people.

The last 30 years have seen improvements in the status of Indigenous Anglicans within the Church. An Anglican Council of Indigenous Peoples oversees Indigenous ministries and justice work. A healing fund supports programs in Indigenous communities. In 1993, the Primate, Archbishop Michael Peers, made a formal apology for the harm done by the residential schools system.

However, the plight of Indigenous peoples within Canadian society as a whole continues to be a national disgrace. There are high rates of violence, crime, incarceration, unemployment, and suicide. The legacy of residential schools is often cited as a significant contributor to these problems. The government and the churches have been slow to respond, and in frustration, many Indigenous people are turning to the courts. This is proving to be painful and costly for both plaintiffs and defendants and, many fear, may not result in healing or in reconciliation. Suggested alternative approaches include "truth telling" and "truth receiving," formal and personalized apologies, compensation or reparation, and memorialization of people's experiences. The Anglican Church is committed to pursuing alternatives to litigation wherever possible, acting justly in litigation when necessary, and continuing to work for reconciliation among First Nations and non-Indigenous Canadians.

Homosexuality and the Church

Homosexuality, the role of gays and lesbians in the Church, and same-sex unions have been a subject of discussion in the Anglican Church of Canada for over a quarter-century. In 1976, the House of Bishops of the Anglican Church of Canada initiated a task force to advise it on the issue of homosexuality in contemporary society and how the Church ought to relate, pastorally and in terms of ordination. In 1979, as an interim measure, the bishops issued a statement based on the following belief: "We believe as Christians, that homosexual persons, as children of God, have a full and equal claim with all other persons, upon the love, acceptance, concern and pastoral care of the Church." As well, the bishops issued a four-point pastoral guideline:

1. Our present and future considerations about homosexuality should be pursued within the larger study of human sexuality in its totality.
2. We accept all persons, regardless of sexual orientation, as equal before God; our acceptance of persons with homosexual orientation is not an acceptance of homosexual activity.
3. We do not accept the blessing of homosexual unions.
4. We will not call into question the ordination of a person who has shared with the Bishop his/her homosexual orientation if there has been a commitment to the Bishop to abstain from sexual acts with persons of the same sex as part of the requirement for ordination.[3]

A number of study sessions were held on the topic of human sexuality throughout the 1980s. In 1991, a new task force was constituted by the Primate. At the 1992 General Synod, a major block of time was devoted to an open forum on the topic. More materials were made available for study.

At the 1995 General Synod, a report was presented that led to a motion affirming the presence and contributions of gay men and lesbians in the life of the Church and condemned bigotry, violence, and hatred directed toward any due to their sexual orientation. This report recommended that the process of dialogue continue and be extended so that the "whole church family has an opportunity to be involved."

At its April 1997 meeting, discussing this topic for the first time in open session, the House of Bishops continued its deliberations and requested that the task force redraft the 1979 guideline in the light of new awareness while, at the same time, retaining the original intent of the guideline. Theological reflection and pastoral action in the Church since 1979 have focused on four key areas: the place of gay and lesbian persons in society; the place of gay and lesbian persons in the Church; the significance of committed sexually active relationships between people of the same sex; and the significance of such relationships for ordination of gay and lesbian persons.

The Anglican Church of Canada believes that gay and lesbian persons are created in the image and likeness of God, and have a full and equal claim with all other persons upon the love, acceptance, concern, and care of the Church. It is on the basis of these theological insights that the Anglican Church of Canada has affirmed that gay and lesbian

---

3 *Statement Regarding the Reporting on the Action of the Anglican Bishops Relating to the Ordination of Persons with a Homosexual Orientation*, 1979, February 27.

persons are entitled to equal protection under the law with all other Canadian citizens.

At the time of the discussions that form the basis of this report, the Anglican Church of Canada, and the worldwide Anglican Communion, maintained its traditional teaching that only the sexual union of male and female can find appropriate expression within the covenant of Holy Matrimony. However, the Anglican Church of Canada does recognize that gays and lesbians form committed sexual relationships, and some congregations within Canada have taken steps toward an acknowledgement of "covenanted" same-sex unions within the Church. In 1998, the Diocesan Synod of New Westminster approved, by a narrow margin, a motion asking their bishop to allow the blessing of same-sex unions. At the time, the bishop withheld consent and initiated a process of study and dialogue on the issue of same-sex unions. The motion was reintroduced at the 2001 Diocesan Synod and approved again, with a greater majority. At the time of the discussions reported on in this volume, the bishop had not released a decision on the blessing of same-sex unions within the diocese.

In June of 2002 — after the completion of this qualitative research — the Synod of New Westminster passed a motion on the blessing of same-sex unions brought before it. This motion asked that the rite of blessing be authorized with the following provisions: a conscience clause ensuring that no person be required to perform or participate in the blessing of same-sex unions; a requirement of a majority vote of approval in any parish wishing to be a place where blessings are performed — otherwise blessings would not be allowed; and the appointment of an Episcopal Visitor to provide pastoral care for priests and parishes who wish it. Despite a walkout of delegates from nine of the diocese's 80 parishes, the bishop assented to the motion, and announced that he would authorize a rite of same-sex blessing.

The Book of Common Prayer, the Book of Alternative Services, and the Future of the Liturgy

The language of worship and ritual has great meaning and significance to many Anglicans. Canadian Anglicans use two worship books — the *Book of Common Prayer* and the *Book of Alternative Services*. The *Book of Common Prayer* has evolved from rites of the 16th century and uses language of that century. Many people continue to find its measured cadences attractive, and it remains the Church's official prayer book. Others prefer the *Book of Alternative Services*, which was published in 1985 as an alternative to the standard text, and is based on the insights of the ecumenical liturgical renewal movement. Its language is more contemporary and draws on a broad range of traditional resources being recovered and developed in many parts of the Anglican Communion. In many parishes, the "alternative" has virtually replaced the *BCP*.

As well, some Anglicans seek further options: liturgies that employ language that is not gender specific, or that include a wider range of images for God, or that draw on the many rich liturgical resources of the Anglican Communion and on ecumenical worship resources.

Diversity in Worship and in Culture

There were two main stages in the spread of Anglicanism — the first in the 17th century, during the colonization of the United States, Canada, Australia, New Zealand, and South Africa. The second stage began in the 18th century, when missionaries travelled to Asia, Africa, and South America to spread the Gospel and to establish churches.

Worship is at the very heart of Anglicanism. Its styles of worship vary from the simple to the elaborate, from evangelical or Reformed to Catholic, from charismatic to contemplative, depending on the tradition and preferences of the individual congregation. Throughout the Church's history, Anglican worship has been expressed in the contemporary language of the people to enable their full participation, and is based on ancient forms.

Canada is a nation of people who have come from many countries. Some of the earliest immigrants from Great Britain brought to this country the Anglicanism practised in the land of its origin. More recent immigrants from countries where the Anglican missions have founded church communities have brought to Canada many different styles and traditions of Anglican worship, born out of the mission church experience and influenced, as is the way of the Anglican Communion, by the language and culture of those countries. Canada, with its multicultural society, has seen the reunion of many different strands of the Anglican Communion, brought together in one national Church. In addition to English, Anglican worship in Canada is conducted in many other languages, including French, Spanish, Cantonese, Japanese, and Mandarin, as well as Indigenous languages.

The BC Referendum on Treaty Negotiations

In the spring of 2002, the British Columbia government announced a referendum on principles for treaty negotiations with First Nations. The referendum asked voters to approve the adoption by the government of eight principles:

1. Private property should not be expropriated for treaty settlements.
2. The terms and conditions of leases and licences should be respected; fair compensation for unavoidable disruption of commercial interests should be ensured.
3. Hunting, fishing, and recreational opportunities on Crown land should be ensured for all British Columbians.
4. Parks and protected areas should be maintained for the use and benefit of all British Columbians.
5. Province-wide standards of resource management and environmental protection should continue to apply.
6. Aboriginal self-government should have the characteristics of local government, with powers delegated from Canada and British Columbia.
7. Treaties should include mechanisms for harmonizing land use planning between Aboriginal governments and neighbouring local governments.
8. The existing tax exemptions for Aboriginal peoples should be phased out.

On April 7, 2002, the Anglican bishops of British Columbia issued a pastoral letter, in which they stated that the referendum as framed and conducted by the government raised serious questions, among them: Should the rights of a minority be subject to a vote by the majority? Is the referendum a true referendum? Is it proper for a government to declare that the results of such a ballot be binding, no matter how many of the electorate cast their vote; and will this referendum enhance or harm the process of treaty negotiation?

The bishops referred all Anglicans to the recommendations of an Anglican task force that urged a "no" vote, or a protest vote. They stressed that the decision on how to vote was "a matter of individual conscience," but they urged Church members "to study and learn about the complexities of treaty claims and negotiations" and emphasized the Anglican task force's recommendations. The 18-member task force recommended to Anglicans that if they chose to participate in the referendum, they should vote "no" to all questions. If they chose not to participate, they should register a protest rather than spoil their ballots.

The People: Stained Glass, Sweet Grass, Hosannas, and Songs

Those who participated in this phase of the intentional listening process brought to it what several described as "the best of Anglican tradition" to their participation. They came with a respectful attention to the stories of others, they came understanding the many faces of the Anglican Church in Canada, and most came wanting to both share their own ideas and learn from others.

While rarely in complete accord with the underlying question of what it means to be an Anglican in Canada today, they came to participate as members of a faith community. Some brought their treasured experience of traditional worship, buildings, and rituals. Some brought rich diversities of culture and language, and their varied perspectives and imperatives. Some brought their passionate and exuberant faith. Some brought their need to "make a joyful noise unto the Lord."

They all came, with spirited energy, eager to help to build a strong Church that will serve spiritual needs today and into the future. And, in the best Anglican tradition, they didn't always agree on the path to be taken, but they did agree to disagree and, in this way, keep the dialogue open and challenging.

I.
STUDY BACKGROUND

1.0 PURPOSE OF THE RESEARCH

In 2001, the General Synod of the Anglican Church of Canada passed the following resolution: "To initiate and oversee a process of intentional listening to the Church in the dioceses and parishes regarding the future life and work of the Anglican Church of Canada, with ongoing monitoring during the next triennium, and recommendations for future planning to come to General Synod 2004."[1]

The Council of General Synod assumed the responsibility of fulfilling this mandate and ensuring that the work required by the resolution was completed.

After careful consideration, the Council decided to use social research, in two phases, at the beginning of the intentional listening initiative. The social research phases of this work consist of a qualitative, exploratory study, to be followed by a quantitative survey. Both of these research studies are to be completed by the fall of 2002. The results of this research will be used to help determine the most appropriate "next steps in the listening initiative."[2]

This report reviews the qualitative research portion of this work. The results of this qualitative work will be used to identify the range of opinions within the Anglican Church community, and to develop a survey that will provide insights into the weight of these opinions among various stakeholders within the Church.

2.0 OBJECTIVES OF THE RESEARCH

- To "listen intentionally" to the wants and needs of the grassroots members of the Church so as to be able to incorporate this

---

1 For an outline of the Anglican Church of Canada's Strategic Plan, please consult Appendix C.

2 For more detailed information on the intentional listening process and the qualitative research conducted in the production of this report, please consult Appendix D.

information into the Church's upcoming strategic planning process
- To engage various grassroots stakeholders in the "intentional listening" process so as to build interest and commitment
- To gain deeper insights into the interests, behaviours, and attitudes of Anglicans
- To use the results of this research to develop a survey instrument to gain a quantitative understanding of these issues among the general Anglican population

3.0 STATEMENT OF LIMITATIONS

The objectives of this phase of the research initiative are exploratory and therefore best addressed qualitatively.

Qualitative research provides insight into the range of opinions held within a population, rather than the weights of the opinions held, as would be measured in a quantitative study. The results of this type of research should be viewed as indicative rather than projectable.

The intent of this research is to provide insights into the range of issues and opinions, and not the weight of those issues, among the general Anglican population.

4.0 INTENTIONAL LISTENING: RESEARCH APPROACHES

4.1 Intentional Listening

There are no rules that define intentional listening, as it is a concept rather than a fixed process. The phrase itself is often attributed to Jacob Needleman. He writes, in *A Little Book on Love* (1998):

> Simply put, there is nothing, nothing in the world, that can take the place of one person intentionally listening or speaking to another.

Generally, those who write about the concept of intentional listening agree that there are some fundamentally important differences between the act of listening with intention and other ways of hearing what others have to say. They suggest that when most people "listen" to what others have to say, their listening abilities are often impeded by an overlay of their own personal agenda. In short, they listen through a filter of their own context, and, in so doing, may "miss hearing" what others have to say.

Intentional listening is a commitment to try to understand the context of others rather than make an evaluation of one perspective over another. The benefit of an intentional listening process is that it is a consciously disciplined attempt to ensure that the issues that are of importance to the person communicating them are not filtered too heavily through the experience and expectations of the listener.

The value of intentional listening is anchored in the belief that the perspective of individuals in a community has meaning and importance, and that it is vital and relevant to the future of the community.

The intentional listening process mandated by the General Synod, of which this qualitative research is one part, will include, over time, both qualitative and quantitative survey research as well as formal meetings, informal conversations, and both formal and informal dialogue.

Environics Research Group was selected by the Anglican Church to provide a detached, outsiders' view of the current context, though the development, execution, and evaluation of the qualitative and quantitative phases of this work.

The results of this qualitative research phase are just a beginning, in support of the Church's strategic planning review.

- This qualitative research provides insights into the range of issues and ideas held within the Anglican Church community.
- The survey work will provide an understanding of the weight that each of these issues and ideas carries within the population of the Anglican Church across Canada.
- The other meetings, discussions, and dialogue will provide opportunities for sharing ideas, concerns, and vision.
- The activities of this intentional listening process will provide tools to be used in setting the path for the Anglican Church strategy for the future.

4.2 The Qualitative Research Phase

This report reviews the qualitative research phase of this intentional listening process.

The intent of this phase of the intentional listening process was to ensure that the voice, perspective, and context of Anglicans across Canada be heard and then respectfully shared with others in the Anglican community. The results of this study are intended as a tool for all Anglicans in considering the development of the strategic direction of the Church as it moves into the future.

Rather than starting with a pre-determined set of questions, this research was specifically designed to provide an open framework for discussion, thus allowing issues, concerns, and visions to emerge.

This qualitative snapshot provides insights into the range of opinions held by Anglicans in Canada at a specific point in time. A survey conducted in September 2002, based on the issues, ideas, and visions shared by members of the Anglican Community in the qualitative phase, provides an understanding of the weight of these opinions among Anglicans across Canada.

4.3 Qualitative Research Approaches Used

Several qualitative approaches were employed in the execution of this project:

- Observation and active listening were used in gaining information and insights with those participating in a session with the Council of Indigenous Peoples
- A traditional focus group approach was used in some sessions among clergy and parishioners
- A workshop approach was used in some sessions with clergy, parishioners, and when engaging the Council of General Synod and the members of the Huron Youth Synod in discussions related to the question areas

5.0 SUMMARY OF PARTICIPATION

5.1 Participation Overview

- Eleven focus groups were conducted, four among clergy and seven among parishioners who are grassroots members of the Anglican Church (as defined in the context of this study). All groups were well attended, and participants came willing and able to contribute to the discussions. Participation was lively in all cases.
- The Anglican Church of Canada managed recruiting and related activities with design support from Environics. Participants for each

group were invited to participate through various networks within the Anglican Church of Canada.

- The size of the clergy and parishioners groups varied from six or seven participants upward to 20 participants.
- Each group was approximately two hours in duration.
- In addition to the 11 focus groups, two Councils of the Anglican Church of Canada and one youth synod were included in the process, through workshops conducted with the full participation of each body:

  —The Council of Indigenous Peoples: approximately 20 participants
  —The Council of the General Synod: approximately 45 participants
  —The Huron Youth Synod: approximately 42 participants

- Sally Preiner, Senior Consultant, Qualitative Innovation, at Environics Research Group, acted as facilitator for all of the sessions.

5.2 Summary of Qualitative Research Approaches Employed in this Study

5.2.1 Small Format Workshop and Focus Group Sessions (2 hours per session)

- These focus group discussions were conducted using either a traditional focus group approach or the Intensive/Interaction Workshop Method.[3]
- The decision to use one format over another was based on the size of the group, as well as the configuration of the meeting room provided. In some cases, the room was simply too small to allow for breakout sessions to be conducted productively; in others, the size of the group was too small to permit the effective use of the Workshop Method.
- When using either format, participants were asked to address each issue area, one area at a time.

---

3 For a detailed discussion of the Intensive/Interaction Workshop Method, please consult Appendix D.

- The discussion was then opened to the whole group for consideration.

5.2.2 Large Format Workshop Sessions (2 hours per session)

Council of Indigenous Peoples

- The original intention was to form a "talking circle" to address the key questions in this study. However, when the researcher arrived to conduct the session, the Council was, within their own process, addressing similar issue areas.
- The decision was taken to "intentionally listen" to the circle already in progress, rather than to intervene with questions, which might have been repetitive, or potentially "out of context" with the Council's objectives for their sessions.

Council of General Synod and Huron Youth Synod

- Participants were given the questions/issue areas to be discussed at the beginning of the session in which they would participate.
- They were then asked to discuss these questions/issue areas, working in smaller groups, and then return to share their team's thoughts and comments with the larger group.

5.2.3 The Questions Used to Stimulate Discussion

In all sessions, the following questions were used to stimulate discussion. Questions one and four were the focus of the discussion, while questions two and three were used as a means of digging deeper to gain insights into the participants' sense of context.

1. What are the concerns most talked about?
   — Within the Church?
   — Outside the Church?
   — Is there any relationship between the two?

2. What are the signs of enthusiasm/excitement?
   — Within the Church?
   — Outside the Church?
   — Is there any relationship between the two?

3. What are the signs of decay and despair?
   — Within the Church?

— Outside the Church?
— Is there any relationship between the two?

4. What are the signs of hope and vision?
   — Within the Church?
   — Outside the Church?
   — Is there any relationship between the two?

"Within the Church" was defined as

- within a participant's own, local church community
- within the broader, regional definition of their parish
- within the larger national Church
- within the global Church

"Outside the Church" was defined as

- outside the local church, in the secular community, including how those outside the Church view the Church
- outside the local church, but in the religious community; that is, from the view of those who attend other churches or who come from faith traditions outside Christianity

5.2.4 Who participated in the discussion groups?

All those who participated in both the clergy and parishioners groups were invited to participate by either their parish church office or some other representative of the Anglican Church of Canada.

Council Participants

Those participating from the Council of Indigenous Peoples were made aware of the "intentional listening" process by their representative in the Council of General Synod. They agreed that Sally Preiner, of Environics Research Group, could participate in one of their sessions as a "listener."

For both the Council of General Synod and the Huron Youth Synod, workshops were developed to work within the set agenda for each of the Councils. Arrangements were made to meet with these two groups during their regular and scheduled meetings.

Characteristics of Participants in Clergy and Parishioner Sessions

The following list outlines, in general terms, the characteristics of participants in the clergy and parishioner sessions, by location. More detailed information about respondent context is included in the Key Findings.

- Red Deer, Alberta: One group of parishioners and one group of clergy participated in sessions conducted in Red Deer. They represented various parish churches in Red Deer and from the surrounding area, including urban, suburban, and rural parishes.
- Vancouver, British Columbia: Two groups of parishioners participated; one group of parishioners represented urban Vancouver churches, the other group represented suburban and beyond-Vancouver-area parishes. The group of clergy in Vancouver represented urban, suburban, and beyond-Vancouver-area parishes.
- Toronto, Ontario: Two groups of parishioners participated in the Toronto area; one group of parishioners represented downtown/urban parishes, the other group represented suburban Toronto parishes. The group of clergy represented urban and suburban Toronto parishes.
- St. John's, Newfoundland: Two groups of parishioners participated in the St. John's area; one group of parishioners represented urban parishes, the other group represented suburban/rural Newfoundland parishes. The group of clergy represented urban and non-urban Newfoundland parishes.

II
SUMMARY OF KEY FINDINGS, CONCLUSIONS, AND THOUGHTS FOR CONSIDERATION

1.0 PARISHIONERS AND THEIR CONCERNS

Issue: *Declining population in mainstream Anglican churches*

- Many parishioners from across the country are concerned about the declining population in the Church. They worry that the declining membership creates a threat to the survival of the Anglican Church of Canada, and raises issues about the financial state of health of the Church, and the effects of that state on the individual parishes.
- Fewer parishioners are concerned about the survival of their own local church, as many feel that their own church community is strong enough to survive.
- Some feel that the decline in membership could be solved if the Church could help local church communities to attract more young members.

Issue: *Youth involvement in the Church/youth ministry*

- Few in mainstream churches feel that they are having success in attracting more young members.
- In most church communities, discussions about bringing more young people into the Church revolve around the financial benefits. Many parishioners feel that if they had programs that were attractive to young people, then their parents would follow them back into church participation.
- Much of the discussion is around the need for young families, specifically to help augment the aging populations as a revenue source and as volunteers doing the churches' work.
- A few urban parishioners spoke about the need for special ministry directed toward youth.

Issue: *Growing populations in the evangelical church communities*

- Anglican churches that are more evangelical reported that they have growing church populations, and they are also among the few who reported active and involved youth membership.
- Some who represent mainstream churches feel that the Anglican Church may be "out of date," while others feel that there is something discomfiting about the "entertainment" versus worship argument.
- Many evangelical churches draw their growing populations from outside the Canadian Anglican tradition — some from the offshore mission tradition, some from outside Christian traditions.
- Outreach in these particular church communities is directed toward specific ethnic populations. The church community offers support to new Canadian families within a comfortable cultural context.

Issues: *Multicultural interpretation of Anglicanism*
Diversity, inclusion, tolerance, fragmentation

- Some urban church communities grow their populations through new Canadians who come from a lifelong Anglican tradition outside the Canadian Anglican experience.
- Outreach programs in these urban churches are often less specifically directed to a particular ethnic group, but rather are welcoming and inclusive of those who come from diverse Anglican traditions.
- These church communities often take particular pride in their multiculturalism, and contrast the experience in their own community against that of more mainstream churches.
- Those who come from outside the Canadian Anglican tradition are concerned that they are not accorded the same "value" in the Church. Most feel that the Church needs to recognize the extraordinary value that the Anglican polyglot brings to the Church.
- Many of those who participate in the mainstream, or more conservative/traditional, Anglican churches are uncomfortable with the form and style of worship adopted by their less mainstream counterparts.
- The differences in interpretation of Anglicanism between "born Canadians" and "new Canadians" in the Anglican Church of Canada is an important factor contributing to the sense of "fragmentation" of the Church, a fragmentation that some feel is accelerating.

Issue: *Book of Common Prayer/Book of Alternative Services/changes in liturgy*[1]

- This issue has less to do with the material itself than it does with "what it means to be an Anglican."
- The liturgy, particularly among those who prefer the *Book of Common Prayer*, is seen as a defining feature of being an Anglican.
- Those who come to Canadian Anglican churches from other Anglican traditions feel that perhaps it is time to revisit the issue of different forms of worship and music, to make them more relevant to those who come from diverse Anglican traditions.
- Still others say that the essential forms could be maintained, but that some aspects could be made more contemporary.
- The issue of liturgy is an important factor when a church community considers leaving the Anglican Church.

Issue: *The residential schools litigation settlements*[2]

- Awareness of the settlement issues related to residential schools is centred on the economic impact of the settlement, not on the issues related to residential schools and their impact on Indigenous peoples.
- Many church communities feel "separate" from the issue, and therefore take no ownership in the settlement of the litigation.
- In some church communities, the emphasis is on their own survival. Some are considering leaving the Anglican Church of Canada, as the only way to survive the economic impact.
- Some of those who are considering this issue feel that real and meaningful healing and reconciliation can only come after all litigation between the Anglican Church of Canada and Indigenous peoples is satisfactorily resolved.
- Some feel that "reconciliation" will be even more difficult than "healing," as it will require that both communication and behaviour change in a meaningful way and be conducted between equals.

---

1 For background information on liturgy and the use of the *Book of Common Prayer* and the *Book of Alternative Services* in the Anglican Church of Canada, please consult Appendix E.

2 For background materials and documents relating to residential schools and the issues of litigation, please consult Appendix F.

- Some feel that current communications between Indigenous and non-Indigenous communities exhibit a disconnect between the language of the Church, which speaks about "partnering," and the behaviour of many who represent the Church, which is described as continuing to be "patronizing."

Issue: *Local outreach and social justice*

- Some church communities across the country have taken on outreach programs in their own communities. Many of these reported that there is enormous pressure on their church community, both in terms of money and of volunteers.
- These church communities are concerned that they may not be able to sustain the level of support that they are currently giving.
- They are concerned that the need for their efforts is increasing. They blame government cutbacks in health, education, affordable housing, etc.
- Communities such as these feel that the Anglican Church of Canada and their own dioceses should be more aware of their needs.
- There is debate on the question: Is outreach at the local community level intended to be evangelical, or is it intended to be part of the Church's responsibility to social justice?
- They also feel that there is a largely unfulfilled role for the Church as advocate for social justice, a role that many feel should be the first priority of bishops at the diocesan level and of the national Church.

Issue: *Homosexuality/blessings*[3]

- In churches that have no active gay and lesbian membership, the issue is felt to be "outside" the church community.
- In some urban churches, there is ongoing discussion of homosexuality, the ordination of gay and lesbian priests, and the inclusion of gay and lesbian people in sacraments and in the active life of the Church.
- Gay and lesbian church members are concerned that the "issue" of blessing same-sex relationships may be dominating the discussion, and issues of inclusion are being lost.
- The discussion of the issue of homosexuality and the Church has, in many church communities, centred on discussions of sexual abuse

---

3 For background information on the position of the Anglican Church of Canada with respect to homosexuality, please consult Appendix G.

and residential schools. For some, the two issues are one and the same.

- Some parishioners feel that homosexuality is a sin, and therefore gay and lesbian people should not be "allowed" to participate in the life of a church community.

Issues: *Leadership of the Church out of touch with the concerns of parish churches*
Balance between stewardship and ministry

- Few feel that the national Church is in touch with the needs of those in parish churches.
- Many parish churches, with the exception of those in Newfoundland, feel that they are not even in touch with their own bishops.
- Many indicated that the Church's leadership is "lost" in the business aspects of the Church and is out of touch with the relevant aspects of ministry.
- Many parishioners feel that there is a lack of communication and support from the national Church; that the national Church expects and needs the support of parish churches, in the form of ever-increasing requests for money, but there is no "pay-back" to the parish church. In most but not all cases, the support sought relates more to aspects of ministry than it does to issues of finance.

Issues: *Fragmentation of the Church*
The meaning of Anglicanism

Many of the current concerns centre on what it means to be an Anglican. Is it evangelistic or liberal, is it steeped in tradition or modern and contemporary? Some feel strongly that there must be only one "right way to be an Anglican." Parishioners ask that the Anglican Church of Canada give them clear vision and leadership to manage the vision.

- Some feel that the difference in opinion related to evangelism is a key basis for fragmentation of the Church.
- Some feel that evangelical Anglican churches may foster "closed" communities that are mono-cultural, theologically conservative, and less connected to Anglican "tradition."
- Some argue that the Anglican tradition has been one of inclusion and tolerance of people from different cultures and ethnic traditions, and that the emphasis on conversion that some feel is inherent in evangelical ministries may indeed be teaching intolerance, and supporting cultural isolation.

Some suggested that clear vision and direction are needed from the leaders of the Anglican Church of Canada on many questions related to the future of the Church.

- What is the vision for the future of the Church?
- What commitment will the Church make to being alert, sensitive, mindful, and action focused?
- How will this be managed in a meaningful way that serves this diverse population?
- How will the Church reconcile the different needs of these diverse and multicultural church communities?

2.0 CLERGY AND THEIR CONCERNS

Issue: *Survival of local church communities*

- Clergy say that financial concerns are causing anxiety in many church communities — some are concerned about their own immediate survival.
- Decline in population is a concern even among growing church communities, as they feel that it will have an impact on their own requirements for financial support to the Church.
- Some feel that they could survive as an independent congregation if they were relieved of the expense of supporting the national Church.
- Some active and growing churches are struggling to understand what value the Anglican Church of Canada brings to their local churches.
- Some feel that the national Church is important because it provides a link to worldwide Anglicanism.
- Some feel that they could do a more effective job of managing the day-to-day business of their church if they were able to make independent decisions about the ownership and management of their property.
- Some feel that the diocesan level of the Church is failing to provide the leaders of the national Church with information about important issues at the local level.
- Some feel that they are on their own from a financial viewpoint, particularly in activities related to issues of social justice.

Issue: *Indigenous peoples' issues*

- There is general agreement among clergy that the settlement issue is "out of the hands" of the Church, and is now with the courts.
- Settlement of litigation, and its economic impact on a particular church community, is a topic for discussion, but the discussion is not about Indigenous peoples, and it has nothing to do with healing and reconciliation — it is almost totally defined by its economic impact.
- Many say that their parishioners don't accept "responsibility" for the residential schools situation, and resent the economic implications.
- This separation from the issue makes it even more difficult for many church communities to willingly participate in settlements that they fear may bankrupt them.
- The lack of settlement, and of full disclosure about the impact that any settlement will have on local parishes, has created, at best, frustration, and at worst, mistrust.
- There is also concern among some clergy that healing and reconciliation cannot succeed until litigation is settled.

Issue: *The shortage of younger members in church communities*

- The solution to declining membership most often mentioned by clergy is "to get more youthful people involved in church communities."
- Some feel that the Anglican Church is "old-fashioned" and out of touch.
- Some feel that the evangelical arm of the Church has moved too far toward entertainment, and away from worship, in its attempt to encourage youth to join the Church.
- Some argue that participation in the Anglican Church has always been cyclical. People come and go at different times in their lives.
- Anglican evangelical church communities are more inclined than other churches to feel that they have something of value to offer to young people.
- Traditional, contemporary, and liberal churches are more likely to feel that more young members in their church community would be "good business."
- Most say that their church communities have not had much, if any, discussion about a relevant "ministry" related to youth.

Issue: *Diversity in worship*

- There are fundamental questions among clergy about what is truly Anglican: traditional versus contemporary, evangelism versus liberalism.
- Many feel that the Church should be providing more and better support to clergy as they seek to help their parishes deal with diversity, issues of inclusion, and tolerance.
- Clergy and their congregations are concerned that, without vision and leadership, the increasing fragmentation of the Church may result in the demise of the national Church in favour of congregationalism.
- Most, but not all, clergy feel that there is room in the Anglican Church of Canada for diversity of liturgy and theology.
- Many feel that it is important for the national Church to address these issues, rather than have them "fester" at the local community church level with no resolution.

If it is resolved that Anglicanism takes diverse forms, then this should be said. *If*, on the other hand, there are church communities that fall outside the acceptable form for the Anglican Church, they should be told. Clergy feel that if there are churches that fall into this category, these church communities would likely not find it surprising that they don't "fit" and they would "move on" and become independent congregations.

Issue: *Connection and responsibility*

- Some clergy feel that the Church is very slow to become aware of issues that it should be addressing.
- The key concern of many is the role of their church community related to social justice. Some church communities are struggling under the weight of their responsibility.
- Many feel that the national Church could, and should, play a larger role as an advocate for social justice.

Issue: *Homosexuality*

- In many areas, clergy told us that it is a non-issue in their church community as "there are no gay people in our area."
- Some said that the discussion is embarrassing to them and to others, so it is mostly just avoided.

- A few said that they feel that the subject should never have been brought forward in the first place, as they believe that homosexuality is a sin and has no place in discussions of the Church.
- In these communities, there is no ownership of the issue, and few see that it has any relevance.
- Many urban and suburban clergy feel that this is a highly emotional topic for many and one that is very divisive in some communities.
- While many urban church communities talk about tolerance, tolerance is a long way from inclusion. Some clergy said that there are those in their community who feel it is their Christian duty to be tolerant of different "lifestyle choices," including homosexuality, but that some of their parishioners take the position that it is "going too far" to let "them" into all church sacraments.
- Other urban church communities take pride in being known as "gay-friendly." Their position is that full inclusion of gays and lesbians in the daily life of the Church, in all of its aspects, is right and appropriate.
- Some clergy feel abandoned by the Church on this issue, and feel that they have not been given a clear vision of the Church's position on the topic.
- Some clergy advocate that an individual priest should be able to make a decision to bless a relationship or not, based on his or her own conscience, while others feel strongly that the Church should have a well thought-out stand on the issue.
- Some clergy are concerned that the issue of blessing same-sex relationships has been discussed at the expense of the more important issues of inclusion of gays and lesbians in the whole and active life of their church communities.
- In many of the smaller church communities, homosexuality and sexual abuse has become a single "hyphenated" topic.
- Some clergy feel that they need help to separate the two topics and help to bring the discussion to the table. Some feel that they are ill-equipped to discuss the topic, as they are unsure of their own position on the issue.

Issue: *Church's leaders distracted*

- Some clergy feel that the leaders of the Church have been distracted by the residential schools issue and the issue of inclusion of homosexuals into the active life of the church community.

- Some clergy worry that these two issues have taken such a predominant place in the day-to-day activities of the Church's leaders that they have lost touch with needs and interests related to other key areas of concern.
- Clergy reported that parishioners feel that the Anglican Church of Canada lacks vision, purpose, and leadership.
- Many feel that there are few "answers" from the Church, and that when issues are identified, there is little response or the response is too long in coming.

What has been lost is clear communication between various levels of the Church. This lack of communication is causing, some clergy fear, a breakdown in trust among all levels of the Church, even among parishes in the same diocese. They are troubled by inadequate support to local parish churches from their bishops, and a lack of vision about the future of the national Church. Most feel that without good leadership the Church will not survive, but some worry that the cost of survival may be the loss of liturgical and theological vision.

3.0 STAKEHOLDER GROUPS IN THE ANGLICAN COMMUNITY

3.1 Anglican Council of Indigenous Peoples (ACIP)

Issue: *The key, overriding concern is the survival of individuals, their families and the communities in which members of the ACIP live*

- Finding sustainable economic opportunities for communities is of paramount importance. Many worry that if they are not able to find sustainable economic solutions, their communities will die.
- Alcoholism among adults and gas sniffing among teens and young adults, boredom and despair are often part of the "texture" of daily life, particularly in remote communities.

Issue: *Moving from special status to equal status*

One key issue area is the use of special funds for the North:[4]

- How is the Fund distributed and who makes these decisions?
- To whom is the Fund accountable? And what are the "rules" under which the Fund operates?

Another key issue is concern about what seem to be unfair or uninformed decisions taken by the bishops related to stipends for those who are responsible for various ministries within individual communities of Indigenous peoples.

- Some spoke about entering their work believing that they would "partner" with a priest in bringing the Church to the people of their community, and then finding that the supplies, materials, and equipment that they require to do their job will not be available to them.
- Some told of the stipend being used as a weapon: "I give you your stipend — remember, you owe me."

Issue: *Healing and reconciliation*

Many said that, rather than feeling that this is a time of "healing and reconciliation," they feel that it is a time of abandonment and denial.

- Some feel the imminent settlement of the residential schools litigation is seen by some as an opportunity for "new beginnings."
- Others feel that it won't make a significant difference to the lives of Indigenous peoples, that settlement will be viewed by the House of Bishops as an "end of the problem" rather than as a beginning of a new relationship.
- Most agree that significant positive change must come from the people themselves, not from outside intervention.
- Some look to the Anglican Church to play a meaningful role in this positive change.

---

4 The General Synod of the Anglican Church of Canada funds work in the North through a grant to the Council of the North. The Council of the North was established in 1976 and comprises all bishops of assisted dioceses. The grant is allocated by the Council to assisted dioceses to support the work of these dioceses and their parishes.

- For this to work, some feel that the Church needs to "teach" non-Indigenous peoples to behave differently, not just to speak differently: while the Church speaks of "partnering" with Indigenous peoples, the behaviour of those who represent the Church to Indigenous peoples continues to be patronizing.
- Some suggested it is time to move away from "special status to equal status."

Issue: *Cultural diversity among Indigenous communities*

Two key issues were discussed related to cultural diversity among Indigenous communities:

- Symbols of specific Indigenous communities are often selected to represent all Indigenous cultures. There seems to be a lack of sensitivity toward the diversity of cultures and cultural icons within the Indigenous communities in Canada.
- Care should be taken within the Anglican Church to provide opportunities for Indigenous peoples to share their individual cultural iconography as they feel it is appropriate.
- When the Anglican Church seeks to incorporate the symbols of Indigenous peoples, there should be consultation with members of diverse communities to ensure that the symbols are used in an appropriate and meaningful context.

Issue: *Evangelistic versus traditional/conservative versus liberal*

- Discussions related to both liturgy and theology suggested that the positions on these issues mirror those of the non-Indigenous church communities.
- Generally, members of the ACIP indicated that they believe that, as there is room in the Anglican Church for the diversity of Indigenous cultures and languages, there is also room for diversity in liturgy and theology.
- What is missing is a way for sharing and embracing this diversity as a "gift" rather than as a problem.

Issues: *Moving toward real healing*
Angry community members — "love of victimization"

- Self-determination, consistent non-patronizing interaction with non-Indigenous communities, and strategies for reaching equal, rather than special, status are crucial to the survival of intact, healthy Indigenous communities.

- Some said that many people in Indigenous communities have become so accustomed to being "victims," that it has become part of their identity.
- They feel this identity of victimization needs to be stopped, if a status of equals among equals is ever to be achieved for Indigenous peoples in Canada and in the Anglican Church.

3.2 Council of General Synod (COGS)

3.2.1 Joy, Enthusiasm, Hope, Vision

- Many say that their church communities are defined at least in part by the structures that are the symbol of their church, and that they take pride and joy in them.
- Some feel that that now they hear more people in their own church communities talking about their quest for more or different spiritual direction.
- Some feel that, among those who attend church, many are interested in doing more than taking up space on a pew. This new interest in taking on a more active role in the life of the Church is seen by some to be a "gift."
- While some churches worry about their church community's survival because there are too few young people attending, other churches feel hope and joy because they find themselves with a growing Sunday school.
- Some feel that the Anglican Church is, at this moment in time, more willing than ever to explore new models of ministry, consider new reforms, even to think about new ways of being a church.
- Some feel that the evangelical movement within the Church has moved the whole Church toward a willingness to talk about God and the Gospel more directly.
- Some feel that prayer is no longer only part of the Anglican Sunday liturgy, but is becoming a more meaningful part of people's daily lives.
- Some feel that the Church is beginning to take much needed action in terms of social justice.

3.2.2 Concerns Within the Church/Concerns Outside the Church

- The relevance of the Anglican Church of Canada, including styles and form of liturgy and the spectrum of theology (evangelical or traditional, conservative or liberal) are often discussed.
- Issues of social justice: cutbacks in government spending, and how best church communities might help, are key issues for some.
- Cutbacks in the number of Anglican Church communities worry some, as do changes in the service of priests in some areas.
- Some, but not all, communities are worried about money and the impact of economic pressure on the survival of the Anglican Church.
- Church communities worry that often there is a "hole" in their communities' populations — from teens through young adults.
- Many worry that if their church community is unable to attract "youth," then it will surely die off.
- Some feel that the key reason for fewer young people in the Anglican Church is that the Church is not relevant to young people.
- When asked directly, some indicated that their own church community has talked about separating from the Anglican Church of Canada.
- Some are concerned that the Church has lost the proper balance between stewardship and ministry.
- A few feel that the Anglican Church of Canada is now all about the business of the Church, while the church communities that are part of the Church have been abandoned to figure out questions of ministry on their own, with little leadership and vision.
- In most church communities, the issues of residential schools, misconduct, sexual abuse, drugs, sex, homosexuality, family breakdown, etc., are not currently being discussed.
- For many, it is not that these topics are considered inappropriate or that they are not worthy of discussion; it is that they are uncomfortable topics to address.
- Some told us that, as priests, they didn't have the skills or "tools" to address these issues with their congregations; without the tools, some don't feel comfortable "teaching" without vision and guidance.
- Many feel that leadership training is needed for both clergy and laity to help them to be more professional in their approaches to sensitive subjects.
- Homosexuality, the inclusion of gays and lesbians into the daily life of the Church, the ordination of gays and lesbians, gays and lesbians and the sacraments within the Church, and the blessing of same-sex

relationships are open topics of discussion only in large urban churches.

- In many other church communities, the topic of homosexuality is not about inclusion, but rather gets linked either to discussions about residential schools litigation or sexual abuse.
- Some feel that a positive decision related to the blessing of same-sex unions would be a dramatic step toward a vision of inclusion and tolerance.

3.3 Huron Youth Synod

Many teens indicated that they were "listeners" rather than active participants in the conversations within their own church communities. Most feel that the ideas and thoughts of young people are not very important to the adults in their church communities.

They talked about their own activities and experiences, and those of youth in general, within their church communities:

- The involvement of youth in their church community includes teaching Sunday school, singing in the choir, and helping with programs for "younger kids." Only a very few churches have active youth programs, events, or classes.
- Many of the Huron Youth indicated that their congregations (adults) were talking about how they might get more young people into the church community.
- Some communities have discussed hiring youth outreach workers or raising funds to support programs for young people, but that the "problem" is that there just aren't that many young people who would want to come to an Anglican Church program. The reason for this, from the teens' perspective, is that if they are involved in a church already, it is probably because of their family's choice of church or because they have already chosen to attend activities at other churches.
- Some reported that they are actively involved in Christian youth programs run by other (often evangelical) churches in their area.
- Some reported that it is great fun to socialize with other Christian teens who share the same interests and values. They went on to say that, while they enjoy this social time, it is not "worship."
- Most worship at an Anglican church along with other members of their families.

What teens want:

- To be respected within their church communities
- To be participants more often than observers
- To see more church-related/sponsored events and activities geared to teens, but not necessarily in their local community church
- To have more opportunities to meet other Anglican teens, to share ideas and fellowship

4.0 THE FUTURE OF THE CHURCH: THOUGHTS FOR CONSIDERATION

Clergy and parishioners alike expressed a need for communication, leadership, and vision from the national Church, on issues both internal and external to the Church.

Parishioners seek guidance, direction, and vision on many issues they see as key to the future of the Church:

- Issues of liturgy and the form and style of worship
- The role of the Church in issues of social justice, and the relationship between the national Church and local parishes in organizing and maintaining outreach programs
- The place of Indigenous Anglicans within the Church: moving from special status to equal status, and erasing the disconnect between language of partnership and patronizing behaviours
- What does it mean to be an Anglican: evangelistic, liberal, traditional, contemporary — one or all?

Clergy are also concerned about lack of communication, direction, and guidance:

- Lack of skills or "tools" to address issues such as residential schools and the impact of litigation/settlement, misconduct, sexual abuse, drugs, sex, homosexuality, and family breakdown
- The need for a clear vision of the Church's position on the of homosexuality
- The need for leadership related to the decline in population in many congregations, and the issues of ministering to youth, and bringing youth to the Church

- Issues of difference in liturgy and worship, diversity, inclusion, tolerance

Parishioners and clergy alike seek increased communication, and new tools to meet the needs of congregations across Canada:

- Leadership training is needed for both clergy and laity to help them to be more professional in their approaches to sensitive subjects
- Ways for congregations with similar needs and interests to freely communicate, share ideas, and work toward solutions

Aspects of the role envisioned for a revitalized Church include:

- The Anglican Church of Canada would take a "front page" position related to issues of social justice
- The Anglican Church of Canada would act as a conduit for information sharing across Anglican communities of faith
- The Anglican Church of Canada would be mindful of the diversity within the Anglican Church and would seek to share the value of this diversity rather than to foster continued debate and deliberation

And most of all:

- The Anglican Church of Canada needs to hurry up. The speed at which decisions and deliberations are made is, in many cases, unacceptable to individuals and church communities that struggle with the issues.

III
KEY FINDINGS

1.0 THE ANGLICAN CHURCH AND COMMUNITY

While the larger part of this report deals with concerns expressed about circumstances both within and outside church communities, no snapshot of these communities would be true if it did not include expressions of the joy, excitement, hope, and vision that are also part of the fabric of communities in the Anglican Church.

1.1 A Snapshot of Anglican Church Communities: April/May 2002

1.1.1 Within the Church: Joy, Excitement, Hope, Vision

Above all else, belonging to a community, particularly a community of faith, is important — even vital — to those who came to share their ideas in this "intentional listening" initiative.

Each community shares a sense of history. Their secrets, both joyful and shameful, are shared rather than buried within the community. In every discussion, "gossip" was near the top of their lists of things that are talked about within the Church.

While there is no question that gossip could be viewed as, and sometimes is, malicious and hurtful, most laugh out loud when they consider the natterings of those in their community. In most communities, the word "gossip" really describes "oral history." Falling in love or lust, marriage and divorce, births and deaths are all chronicled through the telling. In the course of sharing this information, people have an opportunity to examine their own beliefs and values. Some learn through the experiences of others — compassion, forgiveness, and joy in dire circumstances. Some also learn tolerance. Some are introduced to ideas and concepts that would otherwise not enter their lives. Some learn to embrace diversity in all manner of things, where before they didn't know that diversity existed.

Many feel a sense of security from being part of a community. They are there to help others in times of need. The help they offer comes in physical, emotional, and spiritual forms. In return, most believe that if they find themselves in need of help, their church community will be there for them.

For many, fellowship among community members goes well beyond "an hour on Sunday." For some, their church community is at the centre of their lives. It is not surprising that these parishioners and clergy sometimes feel protective of their community against newcomers and outsiders who may come into it and seek to change it. They experience their church community from a very different perspective than those who are less involved.

While most only have the opportunity to experience community through their own church, some have an awareness of the national and even global community of Anglicans. Some have this awareness because they come to Canada from other countries where they have been part of this bigger Church. Others have travelled and discovered the depth and breadth of their shared experience.

Among the joys expressed in urban centres is that the Anglican Church has history and tradition that includes forms of Anglicanism from around the world. For some, this is a sign of the "gift" of multiculturalism that Canada has been given. For others, being made aware of the diversity of traditions within worldwide Anglicanism brings with it the not always welcome prospect of change.

Change is often difficult for people, and it must be remembered that it is people who make up the church communities that are represented in this report. Change has both a dark and a light side.

On the light side of change, new people, growing church community, new music, and new opportunities for outreach were all mentioned as signs of hope and vision.

On the dark side of change, exactly the same list is created. New people may bring new and different ideas; growing a church community will surely change it. New music may not provide the same sense of comfort as more traditional music; new opportunities for outreach may require more work from an already stretched congregation.

Clergy struggle to balance and manage change in their own church communities and, as individuals, may also simultaneously be struggling with change, as it may be at odds with their own experience and beliefs.

Clergy in this study reported that they see and experience joy, excitement, hope, and vision as they watch parishioners taking personal initiative inside the Church. Many sense a growing willingness to commit time and skills to the efforts and activities of the church community. Volunteerism is alive and well in Anglican church communities across the country.

Clergy see a generosity of spirit that is expressed in the energy and enthusiasm of church community members, from raising funds to making beautiful and joyful music.

Many parishioners feel that there is renewed pride in being a Christian. They feel that more members of their church community are interested in finding out more about the basics of their faith, and that many more people are prepared to intentionally seek to experience God.

While many congregations feel that they are "missing" teens, young adults, or those 40 and 50 years old from their church communities, some feel that the renewed interest in finding more young people to join their community is a positive sign. Most feel that their community would be healthier if it were more representative of the larger community.

Good music and good celebration are mentioned as "moments" of joy experienced within their church community.

In looking forward, many church communities feel that the financial position of their church communities is growing stronger.

Cell groups, Bible study, and retreats were all mentioned as being signs of the renewed interest in the "faith" aspect of the Church. This, some said, is a positive move that takes their local church communities into a better balance between stewardship and ministry.

1.1.2 Outside the Church: Concerns

When addressing this question, parishioners and clergy considered both what is being said about the Church by those who are not part of the church community, and also the secular concerns that are part of the fabric of the world in which we all live.

Across the country, parishioners and clergy reported that they see a heightened awareness and concern for spiritual matters. People are talking more about their personal spirituality. Many said that they feel that more and more people are seeking to have a spiritual connection.

Some feel that this will bring people back to their church communities. Others feel that this is a climate where spiritual seekers will look to find relevant connections to "like-minded people." The concern is that the seeking of like-minded people is not necessarily a path to finding faith.

The state of the Canadian economy in general and the economy of their region are also topics of conversation and consideration outside the Church. Many feel that government cutbacks have created an environment of social injustice. Changes in the standard of living, particularly for the elderly or those most vulnerable, are of concern to those outside the Church. Homelessness, the increased reliance on food banks, and increased costs of education and health care are all-important concerns both within and outside the Church.

There is a decreased trust in governments at all levels, and an increased sign that people are "entrenching" to protect their own survival, both in terms of economics and lifestyle.

The events of September 11th have created an interest in understanding more about the beliefs of Muslims as well as other religions. Concerns about war, Canada's military involvement in Afghanistan and the Middle East, and diminished hopes for world peace are also on the minds of those across the country.

There is concern among some that Canada's position as the only "operating polyglot" may become a thing of the past if immigration laws begin to restrict the flow of immigrants to Canada. There is, among others, a concern that Canada's immigration policy has allowed too many "foreign" ideas to become part of the Canadian culture. Some are talking about how to "get back the old Canada."

Changes in lifestyles, family structure, values, and ethics are also causing concerns outside the church community. The increased numbers of children living in single-parent homes and those living in poverty cause concern for the future of Canada's children.

In British Columbia, the recent referendum on treaties and land rights[1] has caused a heightened awareness and interest in understanding and appropriately managing "Indigenous peoples' issues."

1.1.3 Relevance of the Anglican Church of Canada

Among those who are actively engaged in the activities and daily life of their own church community, there is no concern about the relevance and connection of their community to both the concerns within and outside the church.

But, there is confusion and concern about the relevance of the Anglican Church of Canada.

---

1 For further information on the BC Referendum on Treaty Negotiations, please consult Appendices I and K.

Some feel that the national Church is being consumed by stewardship and the business of the church, and has lost the balance between stewardship and ministry.

There is sympathy for the need for careful deliberations about spiritual matters, particularly those that define and codify what behaviour is, and is not, acceptable. However, some feel that when lifestyles, culture, and even science have defined and codified behaviour in the course of social change, the Church need not do it again. Others feel that the word of God has defined all of these issues for all time, and that surely this must be as clear to the Church hierarchy as it is to an individual of faith.

The core issues are not new: evangelism versus liberalism, traditional versus contemporary. These are layered with a diversity of Anglican "tradition" that spans age and geography. While diversity is broadly recognized as a part of the character of the Anglican Church of Canada, few see how diversity might be part of a vision for the future of the Church.

Many of the current concerns centre on what it means to be an Anglican. Is it evangelistic or liberal, is it steeped in tradition or modern and contemporary? Some feel strongly that there must be only one "right way to be an Anglican." Parishioners and clergy ask that the Anglican Church of Canada give them clear vision and leadership to manage the vision.

2.0 PARISHIONERS AND THEIR CONCERNS

Anglican parishioners from across the country share many of the same concerns, but not always for the same reasons. This section of the report summarizes the key issue areas that are shared by church communities across the country. The summary of parishioners in their communities, which follows this section, provides information about how these issues are defined by the context of each of the communities represented in this study.

2.1 Key Issues for Anglicans: A Snapshot in April/May 2002

Issue: *Declining population in mainstream Anglican churches*

Many parishioners from across the country are concerned about the declining population in the Anglican Church. Many worry that declining membership creates a threat to the survival of the Anglican Church of Canada. Fewer are concerned about the survival of their own local church, as many feel that their own church community is strong enough to survive. Some are concerned that the survival of their church community may have to happen without the benefit of the church building in which they now worship.

Declining membership is a concern because it means that the financial health of the Church is dependent upon the numbers of people who feel themselves committed enough to the Church to give financial support.

Some feel that the decline in membership could be solved if, somehow, the Church could help local church communities to attract more young members. Many said that they observe other denominations having success in getting young people in the door, and then encouraging them to stay and to participate. Few in the mainstream Church feel that they are having success in attracting more young members to their church communities.

While the decline in membership in the national Anglican Church is a concern, most parishioners said that their own church communities are *not* declining. Most feel that their membership is stable; some reported that they have a growing membership, including youth.

Some feel that the imbalance between young and old is the natural course of events for their church communities. They said that we should remember that participation in activities in the Anglican Church is cyclical. They told us that those families with pre-teens and teens have many secular responsibilities that interrupt church attendance. These parishioners believe that young adults will return to church activities when it is time to be married. They will lapse in participation as they set up their homes and begin their lives together. They will return to church participation when it is time to have their children baptized; and then will attend with some regularity through their child's confirmation. Many adults return to church participation when their own children are grown and move away from home. It is expected that the now-adult children will begin the cycle again when they marry.

Some feel that, while the cyclical aspect of church attendance may have been true in the past, it is less likely now that the cycle will continue. Many of those who are concerned about the cycle being broken feel that, perhaps, the Anglican Church may not be offering young people what they want from social or spiritual experience. Other churches may be more in touch.

Issue: *We need more youth in the Church*

In most church communities, discussions about bringing more young people into the Church revolve around the financial benefits that young people bring to the church community. Many feel that if they had programs that were attractive to young people, their parents would follow them back into church participation. Much of the discussion is around the need for young families, specifically to help augment the aging population as a revenue source and as volunteers doing the churches' work.

> "I think we want their money. We don't really want the joy of young people in our midst. I know that money is important, but it feels like the wrong reason to go after young people." *Man, urban St. John's*

In many church communities, the discussion about finding and attracting "youth" to the Church centres on marketing the Church to youth. Some parishioners reported actively looking "at the competition." Many feel that the charismatic and evangelical churches have "better music" and that young people have "more fun" there than they might find at a mainstream Anglican Church.

> "Also, I don't think that the type of service that young people would enjoy is the type of service that many of our people want. I think that the Anglican Church is more for older people than for the young.

It hasn't always been that way, but the world has moved on and our Church has just stayed put." *Man, Red Deer*

A few urban parishioners spoke about the need for special ministry directed toward youth. These few parishioners feel urban youth are in need of special attention that is not available to them in most church communities' activities and events.

Issue: *Growing populations in the evangelical church communities*

While mainstream churches worry about declining populations, the Anglican churches that are more evangelical reported that they have growing church populations, and they are also among the few who reported active and involved youth programs. Some who represent mainstream churches look at the evangelical churches and feel that the Anglican Church may be "out of date," while others feel that there is something discomfiting about what they see more as "entertainment" than as worship.

Population growth in the more evangelical churches is across all ages. Most seem to be centred on the value of family and community, and through this context, aspects of theology are introduced.

Many evangelical churches draw their growing populations from outside the Anglican tradition, some from outside Christian traditions. Some are deliberate extensions of mission work outside Canada, and many have more in common with their offshore mission counterparts than with the mainstream Canadian Anglican tradition. Outreach in these particular church communities is directed toward specific ethnic populations. The church community offers support to new Canadian families within a comfortable cultural context.

Some have suggested that these ethnocentric evangelical church communities will move away from their mission roots and closer to the mainstream of Canadian Anglicanism. This seems unlikely. Many members of the Chinese evangelical mission churches are second- or third-generation Anglicans, raised in a mission tradition that is every bit as real as the traditions of Canadian Anglicans, or those from the Caribbean. The mission tradition *is* the style of worship that is now, and will likely remain, the tradition of these church communities.

Issues: *Multicultural interpretation of Anglicanism*
Diversity, inclusion, tolerance, fragmentation

Some urban church communities grow their populations through new Canadians who come from a lifelong Anglican tradition, but a tradition that is outside the Canadian Anglican experience. Outreach programs in these urban churches are often less specifically directed toward a particular ethnic group, but rather are often welcoming and inclusive of those who come from any Anglican tradition that is outside the Canadian experience.

These church communities often take particular pride in the multicultural aspect of their congregations and contrast the experience in their own community against that of more mainstream tradition churches in various ways.

> "The Canadian Anglican Church is mono-cultural, male-dominated, and out of touch. The interpretation of the Anglican Church in Canada is very different than it is in other countries. Our church community provides room for the inclusion of the expression of Anglicanism from diverse perspectives." *Man, urban Toronto*

There is a concern among those who come from outside the Canadian Anglican tradition that they are not accorded the same "value" in the Church. Some feel that they are "set apart" from mainstream decisions. While their "special status" is occasionally to their benefit, most feel that the Church needs to recognize the extraordinary value that the Anglican polyglot brings to the Church. They want recognition and equal status with their more mainstream counterparts.

The connection between the leadership of the Church and new Canadians is weak, they said. Communication and discussion about the world view of Anglicanism needs to be opened up to substantive discussion. These discussions would include consideration for variations in forms of liturgy, including music, as well as issues of social justice, inclusion, and tolerance.

Many of those who participate in the mainstream or more conservative/traditional Anglican churches are uncomfortable with the form and style of worship used by their less mainstream counterparts. Some even went so far as to say that these evangelical and "ethnic" churches are not really Anglican.

The differences in interpretation of Anglicanism between "born Canadians" and "new Canadians" in the Anglican Church of Canada are an important factor contributing to the sense of "fragmentation" of the Church, a fragmentation that some feel is accelerating.

Issues: *Financial concerns/survival of the Church/church closings*
The residential schools litigation settlements

While there is keen awareness of the settlement issues related to residential schools, this awareness is centred on the economic impact of the settlement, not on the issues related to residential schools and their impact on Indigenous peoples.

Many church communities feel "separate" from the issue, and therefore take no ownership in the settlement of the litigation. In some parishes, the emphasis is on their own survival. To establish their "separate right of survival," some are considering leaving the Anglican Church of Canada to be to stand as a separate church community. For some, this seems to be the only way to survive the economic impact.

> "We can pay our own way, but we don't have enough money left for all of the demands from the Anglican Church of Canada. We need to protect our own community first. We have talked about it at length, and we don't feel that we are getting any real benefit from being part of the Anglican Church of Canada. I doubt that they would even notice that we are 'missing.' We are a very small community. We can raise enough money to keep the roof over our heads, but that is about it." *Man, rural Red Deer*

> "We hear about all the money that the Church will have to pay for the residential school lawsuit, and we hear about closing of churches in different places in Canada and on the island. This is Newfoundland; we know about financial hardship here. We have had our fisheries cut back or closed, processing plants shut down. We know why these things happen, but if they are going to close our church, then we will have to find another church. We would rather just stay put, though; so if we can save this ourselves, we will. Not many of us will just move over to some other church, even if it is an Anglican church." *Woman, rural St. John's*

Issue: *Local outreach and social justice*

Church communities are feeling stress, pressure, and vulnerability from the increased demands on their limited resources, both financial and human. While most feel that the church community's responsibility is to provide real physical assistance where and when it is possible, they also feel that there is a largely unfulfilled role as advocate for social justice. Many feel this role should be the first priority of bishops at the diocesan level and of the national Church.

With the exception of British Columbia, where the archbishop has recently made a statement about the referendum on land claims,[2] most don't feel that the Church is taking a stand. Although some did not agree with the archbishop's position, most welcomed the fact that he did take a stand.

Some church communities across the country have taken on outreach programs. Many of these church communities reported that there is enormous pressure, both in terms of money and of volunteers, to support their programs. These churches are supporting food banks, looking for affordable housing, providing life-skills training and parenting programs, and fundraising. Many of these programs are provided in co-operation with other organizations. The objective is solely to provide a bridge of assistance for those who need services that are no longer supported by any level of government. While many of these initiatives were originally conceived as "temporary," more and more communities are counting on these programs. Their status has become "permanent."

These church communities are concerned that they may not be able to sustain the level of support that they are currently giving, and they are further concerned that the need for their efforts is increasing. They blame government cutbacks in health, education, affordable housing, and other services for the current circumstances.

Church communities who are engaged in such programs reported that they feel that the Anglican Church of Canada and their own diocese should be more aware of the needs in individual communities. They seek vision and support from both their local and the national Church. Most see these efforts as their church communities' responsibility to the wider community, not as part of an evangelical effort. Most feel that this is an important differentiation, as it allows help to go to those of many faiths and backgrounds.

> "Some of the other churches in town only help particular people who are willing to 'be saved' by their church. We don't do it that way. But it makes you wonder. They seem to have growing numbers,

---

2 For further information on the response of the Church in British Columbia to the referendum, please consult Appendix J.

> and we don't. Maybe they have the right idea. I don't think it would be the Anglican way, now would it?" *Woman, urban St. John's*

Some feel that, perhaps, outreach should be part of an evangelical mission, with those receiving help somehow "obligated" to participate in the church community. Others feel that this evangelical "requirement" would not be within the true spirit of Christianity.

In seeking vision and direction, many would like to see the Church take a stand on the question: Is outreach at the local community level intended to be evangelical, or is it intended to be part of the Church's responsibility to social justice?

Issue: *Homosexuality/blessings*

Generally, unless the church community is "gay friendly," the issue is side-stepped or avoided whenever possible. In some urban churches, there is ongoing discussion of homosexuality, the ordination of gay and lesbian priests, and the inclusion of gay and lesbian people in sacraments and in the active life of the Church. In most other churches, many parishioners said the "issue" was discussed "a few years ago, but not much since." Among churches that have no active gay and lesbian membership, the issue is felt to be "outside" the church community.

Among gay and lesbian participants in this discussion, there is some concern that the issue of blessing same-sex relationships may be dominating the agenda. For many of those in the gay and lesbian community, issues of inclusion are thought to be of paramount importance. Many feel that if issues of inclusion could be resolved, then the blessing of relationships would follow naturally.

The discussion of the issue of homosexuality and the Church has, in many church communities, centred on discussions of sexual abuse and residential schools.

Many parishioners in suburban and rural church communities reported that the topic is one that makes people uncomfortable, so they just don't talk about it at all.

> "Well, we don't live in an area where there are any gays, so it doesn't have anything to do with us, really." *Man, suburban Vancouver*

When asked if their church community would welcome gay and lesbian people into the congregation, some thought that their community would be welcoming. Others thought that their community would not be a comfortable place for a gay or lesbian person to worship. A few feel that homosexuality is a sin, and therefore gay and lesbian people should not be "allowed" to participate in the life of a church community.

Issue: *Interfaith dialogue*

In some urban church communities, opening interfaith dialogue has been important following the September 11th terrorist attack on the United States.

Where there has been an attempt at interfaith dialogue, church communities report that there is a growing spirit of tolerance, and an awareness that there are more things that people share in common than things that make them different from one another.

Issue: *Leadership of the Church is out of touch with the concerns of parish churches*

Few feel that the national Church is in touch with the needs of those in parish churches. Many parish churches, with the exception of those in Newfoundland, feel that they are not really in touch with their own bishops. This is true even when members of their parish are represented at synod. Many indicated that the Church's leadership is "lost" in the business aspects of the Church and is out of touch with the relevant aspects of ministry. Some feel that the balance between stewardship and ministry has been lost, and that communication between parish and the national Church on issues of stewardship is insufficient.

> "We talk about declining numbers in our churches, and we are closing some of our old community churches, and yet we are building new churches. This doesn't make sense to me. Who is making these decisions, and why don't they explain to us why they are doing this?"
> *Woman, rural parish, Newfoundland*

Some church communities across the country are considering the drastic step of becoming independent congregations, rather than continuing to be part of a larger organization that some feel is not interested in their survival. Some feel that the Anglican Church of Canada is either unable or unwilling to give them the sort of support or attention that they feel is a "good return on the value of their contribution."

> "Maybe we have had the focus backward for too long. I expect that the Anglican Church of Canada, or the diocese or whatever, will

look after the parish church interests, but that isn't the way it works. The parish looks after the diocese and their needs, and the diocese is just a little too invisible for us to internalize and 'own' what it is that they do." *Man, Red Deer*

In most, but not all, cases, the support required relates more to aspects of ministry than it does to issues of finance. Many parishioners told us that there is a lack of communication and support from the national Church, and that the national Church expects and needs the support of parish churches, in the form of ever-increasing requests for money, but that there is no "pay-back" to the parish church.

Groups within parish churches would like to have access to information that would help them find other parishes with similar circumstances, with which they could share ideas. This is of interest to both those churches who feel that they are being successful in their various efforts and those who feel frustrated or abandoned.

Issue: *Book of Alternative Services/Book of Common Prayer/changes in liturgy*

While most church communities seem to have found a way of accommodating the needs of those who prefer the *Book of Common Prayer* over the *Book of Alternative Services*, it is not always a comfortable accommodation. The issue has less to do with the material itself than it does with "what it means to be an Anglican." The liturgy, particularly when viewed from the perspective of those who prefer the *Book of Common Prayer*, is a defining feature of being an Anglican.

Among other Anglican church communities, there are questions about the "interpretation" of Anglicanism from a traditional white/Anglo-Saxon/male perspective. Those who come to Canadian Anglican churches from other Anglican traditions feel that, perhaps, it is time to revisit forms of worship and music, to make them more relevant to those who come from diverse Anglican traditions.

Among those who have a lifelong experience with the Anglican Church of Canada, some wonder if maybe the Church has grown "old-fashioned." Some said that it isn't much fun to be an Anglican.

Some others said that, while the Anglican Church "may not be the best place to find Christ, it is the best place to grow in Christ." People who feel this way argue that the comfort of the liturgy provides room for growth; while the "entertainment" value of other churches may be more enticing, they don't have the "restful spirit" that is needed for true growth.

Still others said that "the liturgy might be more relevant if it seemed less connected to the 1800s [and more] to the 21st century." They argue that the essential forms could be maintained, but that some aspects could be made more contemporary. They argue that to be contemporary would enhance, rather than detract from, worship.

While most would like to set the issue of the liturgy aside, some said that the issue is very important, but seems impossible to resolve. The issue of liturgy is a key factor in discussions in each church community that considers separating its congregation from the Anglican Church of Canada. It causes distress in some communities. Parishioners seek direction and vision on this issue.

3.0 PARISHIONERS IN THEIR COMMUNITIES

3.1.1 Toronto: Downtown Parishes

Social justice, concerns about the economy/lack of money, sexual abuse in the Church among the most vulnerable, and issues around changes in the liturgy, including discussions about the *Book of Alternative Services* and the *Book of Common Prayer*; were the issues of concern most often mentioned by urban Toronto parishioners.

Issues: *Withdrawal of government support to social services*
Social justice issues/concerns for those less fortunate, homeless

Social justice issues in urban Toronto include concerns for homeless people, as well as more general concerns about the "less fortunate." In urban Toronto, the issue of homelessness is thought to be political, immediate, and urgent. Government cutbacks, in particular cutbacks made by the Province of Ontario in social services, combined with an increase in migration to Toronto by those in search of jobs and decreases in help for those with medical or mental health issues, add pressure to already "stretched" church communities in the Toronto urban core.

Some concern was also expressed that there are fewer or less visible advocates for the poor and the homeless. Some said this decrease in visible advocacy "forces" church communities to take on a more adversarial role than in the past.

Concerns about the economy include some very personal concerns about their own economic well-being (particularly concerns about aging), but most are primarily concerned about others for whom living in the City of Toronto is an economic struggle.

> "When services are cut, it affects everyone in the city." *Man, urban Toronto*

> "We can't keep enough food in our food bank to feed the people we need to feed. Many people among the hardest working volunteers are beginning to feel burned out." *Woman, urban Toronto*

Some parishioners are concerned that the city itself is in economic trouble, that school boards, parks, and programs for children and families are under attack. This concern is deep enough that it is talked about both within and outside of their church community.

***Issue:** Homosexuality and sexual abuse in the Church*

In Toronto, some urban church communities are clearly engaged in discussion around issues of homosexuality. In particular, there is discussion around the blessing of same-sex commitments. Those participating in this discussion who represent the gay community suggested that, while the issue of same-sex commitment celebrations is clearly important, it may have overshadowed other inclusion issues, such as the ordination of gay and lesbian priests and the active involvement of gay and lesbian people in the life of the Church.

> "The blessings issue is important, but I worry that it is now the only discussion. The Anglican Church needs to deal with inclusion issues. If gays and lesbians were really allowed full participation in the life of the Church, then blessings wouldn't be an issue." *Man, gay community, urban Toronto*

Some parishioners from urban Toronto church communities reported that, while the subject was discussed some time ago and still comes up for discussion from time to time, it is not openly discussed; and, indeed, where possible, the issue is "side-stepped" or "skirted." Some said that this "distancing" is the way in which members of their congregation can avoid confrontation on the issue, as the topic tends to be highly emotionally-charged and potentially divisive.

Those who are uncomfortable with the issue were more likely to say that they believe that homosexuality is a sin, and that the Anglican Church should "take a stand" on it.

> "Well, I don't mean to be rude to anyone here, but I have always been taught that homosexuality is wrong. Period! It shouldn't have to be discussed. It is a sin, plain and simple. At our church, we don't understand the fuss." *Man, urban Toronto*

The "issue" of homosexuality is blended into discussions related to residential schools, and other issues that involve Indigenous peoples. Also included in these murky discussions are issues and concerns around "the protection of the most vulnerable," by which they mean sexual abuse of young children, in particular, boys. For some, discussions about issues related to homosexuality are totally intertwined with discussion of sexual abuse.

In this climate of discussion, it is difficult for many, particularly those in traditional conservative mono-cultural church communities, to have any thoughts about issues around the inclusion of gays and lesbians into the broader church community.

Issues: *To use the Book of Common Prayer or the Book of Alternative Services*
How to satisfy those with different preferences

For the most part, discussions about the use of the *Book of Common Prayer* or the *Book of Alternative Services* are "old news." However, there is still ongoing and emotionally charged discussion among some church communities related to the use of the *BCP* or the *BAS*. Most urban parishes have "resolved" the issue by providing different types of services to meet the needs of different parishioners. A few church communities "define" themselves by the predominance of one book over the other.

> "It doesn't feel like worship to me when I attend the 11:00 service. I feel that worship should be traditional, this is respectful. The *Book of Alternative Services* just 'tries too hard' for my tastes. I think that we should never have left the *Book of Common Prayer*." *Woman, urban Toronto*

In some congregations, discussions about the introduction of more secular forms of music and dance have raised concerns. In others, the introduction of new forms of music and dance are considered part of the evolution of the Church and the means by which the Church can "reach out" to those who are not now part of their church community.

> "A real sign of joy for me has been some dance that has been introduced to some of our worship." *Woman, urban Toronto*

> "I think that we must be very careful with all of this music and dance. We need to be mindful of the difference between entertainment and worship." *Man, urban Toronto*

3.1.2 Toronto: Suburban Parishes

While there are many common elements in the issues of concern among urban and suburban Toronto parishioners, there is a difference in emphasis and priority. Youth ministry or youth involvement with liturgy and music, youth programs, aging parishioners, multicultural church community management, and local community outreach were the issues of concern most often mentioned by Toronto suburban parishioners.

Issues: *Young people in the church community*
Changing nature of their own church community population

Some suburban parishioners feel that too much emphasis is placed on the development of youth programs. They said that participation in a church community is "cyclical," that is, people participate in church activities at different times during their lifetime, and that teenagers and young adults are "too busy" to be bothered much with church.

> "I think we spend too much time thinking about the 'youth question.' Anglican Church attendance has always been cyclical." *Woman, suburban Toronto*

Others expressed specific concerns that there are too few young people in their church community. Some worry that if there are no new young adults, there will not be enough money to support the individual community. Some worry that this may mean that their own church may be closed and that their own church community may cease to exist.

> "If we don't attract young people, then who will pay to keep the lights on when we are gone?" *Man, suburban Toronto*

Some in aging Anglo-Canadian neighbourhoods are concerned about the changing nature of the population served by their local church community. Some worry because the population is aging and, as it does, the population of their own church community is decreasing.

Issue: *Youth ministry/youth involvement*

In many of the churches, where there is concern about declining participation by young people in the Church, some feel that the liturgy may be "alienating" younger people. Some feel that today's young people find the church services boring.

> "Well, let's face it. It's not much fun to be an Anglican." *Man, suburban Toronto*

Some argue that they, and the young people they observe in their own congregations, are often looking for "community." Those who believe that the effort should be made to develop programs and activities directed toward teens and young adults argue that, if young people can't find relevance in a church community, then they will leave it. It will be much harder, if not impossible, to get them to come back in the future.

> "I worry that we don't seem to offer what young people want in a church. My daughter and her friends go to a Christian youth group at an evangelical church. I'm honestly worried that we will lose her forever. She has a wonderful time at this other church. Lots of young people participate in their programs. This makes me think that church-going doesn't have to be cyclical. It just needs to be meaningful." *Woman, suburban Toronto*

In an attempt to counter this sense of "alienation," some churches are developing or considering the development of a specific outreach program aimed at teens and young adults in their geographic area.

Some mentioned that youth ministry provides an opportunity for the Anglican Church to be present and relevant to non-Anglicans in the community. These people reported that, within their own church community, many feel that there is a need for greater commitment to issues of social justice, more need to be "in touch" and "socially relevant."

Some also feel that to do this will require more dedicated and disciplined approaches to outreach. In this case, outreach is not directly or overtly linked to evangelism. Some, but not all, feel that such outreach should be more overtly evangelistic.

Issue: *Fragmentation of the Church*

Some feel that the difference in opinions concerning evangelism is a key basis for fragmentation of the Church.

> "We are what you would call a traditional Canadian Anglican church. I suppose that you could say we are 'white-bread.' This Bible thumping that some of our churches do these days is embarrassing." *Man, suburban Toronto*

Some feel that those Anglican churches that are evangelical may also foster "closed" communities that are mono-cultural, theologically conservative, and less connected to Anglican "tradition."

> "Eighty per cent of our membership, maybe more, is Chinese. We have a mission church tradition. We have our own way of doing things." *Woman, suburban Toronto*

Some go so far as to argue that the Anglican tradition has been one of inclusion and tolerance of people from different cultures and ethnic traditions, and that the emphasis on "conversion," which some feel is inherent in evangelical ministries, may indeed be teaching intolerance and supporting cultural isolation.

> "In our church community, we have people from all over the world. We are very proud of that. This is the Canadian Anglican tradition, to welcome and include newcomers, particularly if they come from another country where they have Anglican churches. Some of these mission churches aren't like us at all. They have people from only one country. They don't want people from other places to worship with them, and they want to worship in their own language." *Man, suburban Toronto*

There is some concern that that there doesn't seem to be a clear "position" on the part of the Anglican Church related to evangelical activities. Most would agree that evangelical work, both in Canada and outside Canada, is important, but that the specific nature of these ministries, and the Church's vision on tolerance and inclusion, are troublingly unclear.

Issue: *Homosexuality*

In Toronto suburban communities, many reported that the subject of homosexuality isn't relevant in their church communities, as "we don't have any gay people in our church community."

While we were told that there has been discussion about various issues around homosexuality in these suburban churches, most of the suburban parishioners participating in this study reported this issue as "old news," and not a key topic in their current discussions, issues, and concerns.

> "Oh, yes, we talked about that about two, maybe three, years ago. Is there some other news about this that we should know?" *Woman, suburban Toronto*

Among those from suburban churches, some feel that their church community would likely welcome, with tolerance, gay and lesbian persons wishing to join their community.

> "If gay people came to our church, then I'm sure we would talk about it. We are a very tolerant group of people. But in the area where we live, there are no gays." *Woman, suburban Toronto*

More indicated that they feel that it would likely make many people in their community very uncomfortable to know that "gays" were in their church. It is unclear what precisely would be discomfiting, but the indication is that "there are other churches where they can go."

3.1.3 Toronto: Urban and Suburban Parishes — Shared Issues

Issues: *Litigation*
Settlement related to litigation may bankrupt the Anglican Church of Canada
Impact of residential schools on Indigenous cultures
Healing and reconciliation in a time of litigation

The impact of residential schools on Indigenous cultures or their effects on individual Indigenous peoples and their communities, as well as related issues of sexual abuse, are not concerns that are "owned" by many urban or suburban Toronto Anglican parishioners.

> "I've been thinking about this recently. Why do people only talk about sexual abuse when they mention residential schools? It horrifies me that our Church could have been involved in taking children away from their homes. To try to kill off a culture! Doesn't anybody else know about this? Isn't anyone else outraged? I don't think people are really thinking about this issue." *Woman, urban Toronto*

> "When you hear residential school, you think sexual abuse. I know there was more to the story than that, but mostly you hear about the abuse of vulnerable little boys." *Man, suburban Toronto*

Without a sense of ownership of the issue, but with a defensive tone, these parishioners said that "we, the Anglican Church, are not really at fault here, we've been 'third-partied.' It is so unfair." Some said that "it" was discussed "a couple of years ago," and some then wonder "why is it taking so long to resolve?"

While "healing and reconciliation" were mentioned by a few people as being of personal interest or special interest to their urban church community, most said that they are "aware" that healing and reconciliation were discussed in their church community "a while ago."

The tone in reporting this is almost as though "healing and reconciliation" were something to be done at a time around the last Synod, but that that time is "over now and we have moved on to other things." It is interesting to note that one team of participants re-titled "healing and reconciliation" as "healing and reconstruction."

With the exception of a very few inner city churches, where there are Indigenous peoples in the congregation, overall there is only a very shallow depth of understanding around the issue, and little "top-of-mind" awareness.

For most, the "residential schools issue" is, if they think about it at all, an issue of litigation and economic settlement. This viewpoint divorces the issue from being about people, and instead defines the issue to be about legal wrangling, claims, and settlements.

Many are aware and concerned that litigation related to residential schools and "the Indigenous peoples' problems" are potentially a threat to the economic viability of the Anglican Church of Canada. Among both urban and suburban church communities, parishioners reported that the residential schools issue is more likely to be viewed from a position of concern about economic impact, first at their own local church, followed by the economic impact on the Anglican Church of Canada.

Among those who are thinking about this issue, some indicated confusion about the notion of "healing and reconciliation" in a time of litigation. They wonder how it is possible to find any substantive change to the environment with litigation still pending. Participants who expressed this concern indicated that they feel that real and meaningful healing and reconciliation can only come after all litigation between the Anglican Church of Canada and Indigenous peoples is satisfactorily resolved. Only then will it be possible to have healing.

Some feel that "reconciliation" will be even more difficult than "healing," as it will require that both communication and behaviour change in a meaningful way. New ways of communicating between communities must be found.

The issue related to communications between Indigenous and non-Indigenous communities is around the disconnection between the language of the Church, which speaks about "partnering," and the behaviour of many who represent the Church, which is described as continuing to be "patronizing." Patronizing behaviour, some feel, is not in any way connected to the spirit of reconciliation; "reconciliation must be between those who are and who feel equal and are treated with equality."

Issue: *Healing ministry*

While the residential schools issue is one that conjures primarily litigious images, the concept of a "healing ministry" *is* important to many Anglican parishes in the Toronto area. In the urban/suburban Toronto context, a "healing ministry" seeks to reach out to those in need within the urban context. In particular, food banks and shelters for those without adequate housing are two examples given.

> "We are very proud of our lunch program. We make sandwiches that get served around lunch to some of the homeless people in the downtown core." *Woman, urban Toronto*

> "There are more people than ever in need of help in Toronto. People who through no fault of their own are homeless and hungry. We have to do what we can." *Man, suburban Toronto*

Some feel that the Anglican Church should take a stronger stand in terms of social justice, equity, and fairness issues, particularly as these relate to quality of life for those who, for any reason, are economically marginalized.

The local church should also be willing to help those in their own local community, and should be able to count on the Anglican Church of Canada to help as well. Financial support is not the only thing that is seen as "helpful" in social justice issues.

Many in both urban and suburban Toronto church communities feel that the role of social justice advocate is beyond the scope of the local churches, and that this should be one of the primary functions of the "big" Anglican Church of Canada.

> "The head of the Church or the House of Bishops should take a stand. They have power and authority. They should use it to stop all the cutbacks." *Woman, urban Toronto*

The need for a "healing ministry" is important at this time because of the major cutbacks in funding from all levels of government to those people and communities whom the Anglican Church communities seek to help. A healing ministry in this context has to do with a general sense of social inequity and a widening gap between those who have and those who don't.

> "Every time I see a homeless person, I think about how they are really not much different than me. Every time, I wonder what I would do if I were in their shoes. Most of us live pretty close to that edge in Toronto. So today I have a job.... If I lose that, well ....Things are so expensive. I can see how it can happen." *Woman, urban Toronto*

It is important to note that there is a strong sense of pride among parishioners who come from church communities with outreach programs. There is however, in some cases, a tone of smugness, a competitive edge with other church organizations, both in and outside the Anglican Church. Doing "your social duty," for some parishes, is clearly thought of in a competitive manner.

> "Our church feeds more people breakfast than any other in town." *Woman, urban core Toronto, Anglican church community*

> "We have programs for teens in need. Of course, other teens are able to come as well, but it is really for the less fortunate." *Man, youth program director*

Urban and suburban church communities that are recipients of the efforts of more affluent churches, while grateful for the help that they receive, are sometimes made to feel as though they are the patronized "poor cousins."

> "While the churches that help us out should be praised for their generosity, they should not be allowed to use their gifts to us as a way of putting people down." *Man, urban Toronto, mission church community*

Issues: *Life stress and secular commitments*
No day is sacred

There was general agreement that the biggest "competition" that the Church faces is from secular commitments. Young families need to allow their children to participate in sports activities, which are often scheduled on Sundays. Many of those who might participate in Sunday church activities must work on Sunday, or they find that Sunday is the only day when they have time to take care of chores and responsibilities around their homes.

> "Hockey practice for one boy, swimming for my daughter. In the summer, it's softball with my son on Sundays. I don't set the days, we just have to go when the team is scheduled for a practice." *Man, suburban Toronto*

While some argued that "if they wanted to go to church, they would find time," others suggested that perhaps the Church needs to consider more opportunities at other times when people could find fulfilling involvement in the life of the Church and the church community.

Issue: *Stewardship/landholdings/church closings*

In both suburban and urban parishes, participants told us that their local church communities are concerned about how landholdings are managed, and how decisions are made to close one church and to keep another open.

Some feel that the decisions that are made may not take into account sufficient information about the impact of those decisions, both in the short term, related to the church communities affected, and also in the longer term. Some feel that when there is consultation on these issues, it is not substantive; some feel that "consultations" are really "PR efforts, and not consultation at all."

Issue: *The "competition" has better music*

Some parish participants, who describe themselves as coming from church communities with an evangelical approach to worship, worry that perhaps the Church is "behind the times," that there need to be greater diversity of music and more activities appealing to young people. Others feel that making changes to the nature of worship is not appropriate within the Anglican context.

> "How we do our service is the Anglican way to do things. It has always been pretty much the same way as it is today." *Man, suburban Toronto*

Those who argued against the introduction of different musical styles, or the addition of bands and dance, explained that they believe that these forms of worship are acceptable, but not within the traditional forms of the Church. Some feel that these are diversions, acceptable as a Christian-based entertainment, but that entertainment should not disrupt the purpose of worship.

> "I know that some people think that it is all right and modern to have contemporary music and even dance in the Church. We are Anglicans. That sort of music and dance isn't our tradition. I feel that respectful worship is all about tradition. When I hear about contemporary music and dance in church, I am concerned that we are confusing entertainment with worship." *Man, suburban Toronto*

Some said that the issue of newer, more compelling and interesting or relevant music isn't just an issue related to young people. Several mentioned that their teenaged children attend non-Anglican evangelical churches. They too have attended these churches, from time to time, because their teens are part of the choir program.

> "I felt real joy and a spirit of worship when I heard the music. What can be wrong with that?" *Woman, suburban Toronto, lifelong Anglican*

> "I think that most of the music in the Anglican Church was probably pretty 'modern' in its day. What I don't understand is why it doesn't move on now." *Male, urban Toronto, grew up in Catholic tradition and joined Anglican community 20 years ago*

Issues: *Church community is growing*
Worry about having enough room for all of those who attend a service

Other participants from both urban and suburban churches talk with excitement and enthusiasm about the growing number of people who are part of their congregations. A growing population is most often reported in evangelical churches and other church communities serving primarily new Canadians, rather than, as they describe it, "the old guard."

> "Well, in terms of church demographics, our church is certainly growing. We don't fit into our place of worship. We are going to have to build a church soon." *Man, suburban Toronto*

Toronto parish congregations where members of the church community are originally from outside Canada sometimes feel a bit alienated from the national Church. This feeling of separation occurs even in church communities where Anglicanism is the "tradition" in which parishioners have participated throughout their lifetime. They go on to explain that, because the "interpretation" of the Anglican Church in Canada sometimes seems very mono-cultural, the leadership very male-dominated and older than non-Anglo-Canadian Anglicans, they sometimes feel that their own Anglican cultural experience is not represented meaningfully by the Anglican Church of Canada.

Many urban and suburban Toronto area parishioners reported that their specific church community is very important to them. A few said that being part of the worldwide Anglican Church is also important.

Being part of the bigger Anglican Church of Canada is not considered highly relevant by some of those in the Toronto urban core. Some said that they feel that their own spiritual needs and their sense of belonging is related to their local church community, as well as to the wider global Christian community. The Anglican Church of Canada is not really "necessary," as they find that their "needs" are fully met by their local church.

People who attend charismatic and evangelical churches within the Anglican Church are the most likely to report growth in their congregations in the Toronto and suburban area. Those who are members of these particular church communities are also more likely than their counterparts to indicate that they have active youth (13 to 25 years old) involvement, and that their communities include many young families with children between infancy and ten years of age.

Some feel that this is because of the particular set of values that community members bring from various cultural backgrounds. Others feel that the success of these church communities has more to do with "more interesting and lively" services than with differences in values.

Churches in both urban and suburban Toronto who have active youth programs were also more likely than their counterparts to report that they have a growing, rather than a declining, church population.

3.2.1 Vancouver: Downtown Parishes

The referendum on Aboriginal land claims, government cutbacks in social spending, the Anglican Church's role in social advocacy, blessing of same-sex relationships, inclusion of gays and lesbians into local church communities, and the changing nature of church populations, including factors such as aging, immigration, and multiculturalism, were the issues of common concern most often mentioned by urban Vancouver parishioners.

Issue: *Homosexuality*

In urban Vancouver, issues around blessing of same-sex couples,[3] homosexuality in general, and issues around the inclusion of gays and lesbians in the life of a church community were mentioned as key concerns among some parishioners and in some churches.

Among most of the urban parishes represented, participants said that their church community is openly welcoming to gay and lesbian members. However, there are some church communities in urban Vancouver that clearly are not.

Even among those who claim to welcome gay and lesbian people into their community in a spirit of "tolerance," some feel that there "ought to be some limits or rules." Some indicated that these church communities do not openly welcome gay and lesbian people to "drink from the cup" or even to participate as servers.

> During the course of the group discussion, one man explained, "I belong to a church community where I, as a gay man, am not allowed to participate in sacraments, or for that matter, in much else. I stay at this church community because it has always been my church 'home.' I attended the church as a child, and I attend with my parents as an adult. I've been open about being gay, because I am always open about it. I don't want to change my church community; I want my church community to practise tolerance and inclusion. I will fight for this, but it certainly isn't comfortable. I find spiritual comfort with other groups, outside my parish church." *Gay man, urban Vancouver*

> One man said, after the group had closed and we were walking to our cars: "They can come to our church, they can sit and listen, but they should understand that they are different than the rest of us, and just let it be. There are other places where they can go and be with their own kind. I don't believe that sex has any place in church."

---

3 For further information on the debate on blessing of same-sex unions in the Diocese of New Westminster, BC, please consult Appendix H.

The issue of inclusion of gay and lesbian persons in the church community includes but is not limited to the blessing of same-sex unions.

> "We, the gay men and women in the Anglican community, are concerned that the same-sex union discussions put the issues around inclusion on a back burner. Many of us feel that if inclusion was seen as the real issue, and if it was addressed with vigour, it might create an atmosphere that would at least be working towards tolerance. From inclusion and tolerance would come a deeper understanding about the importance of the blessing of same-sex unions for those who seek these blessings." *Gay woman, urban Vancouver*

Issue: *Relevance of the Anglican Church of Canada*

The relevance of the Anglican Church of Canada, and its impact and influence on local church community decisions, was a commonly mentioned concern. In particular, the "rights" of local clergy to independent decisions on issues of stewardship (buying and selling of assets), music, prayer books, and the nature of the "service" and what is to be included/excluded were all mentioned.

The question of the Church's relevance is in part an expression of concern over the viability of the Church as it moves through various litigation proceedings. Some feel that the discussion of relevance is really about the survival of their own church community if it were to become independent from the Anglican Church of Canada.

> "We have talked about this a lot in our church; if the Anglican Church of Canada goes broke, we can make it on our own, no problem. We worry that maybe we don't actually own our church building, and that it could be taken away from us, but as a church community we could survive that." *Woman, urban Vancouver*

The discussion of relevance, for some, includes issues around the liturgy.

> "Our church community is thriving. We are a Chinese evangelical church, and we are quite different than other Anglican churches in our area. Our church community is made up of immigrants to Canada, many of whom don't have a Christian background. They don't have any strong loyalties to the Anglican Church of Canada; most of us don't even really know what it is all about. In fact, we don't have much to do with any other church community. We do

> hear that there are some people who don't approve of our ways. So, we do talk about it sometimes. What does this bigger Church have to do with us and with our community's needs? Some of us wonder if we really belong to this bigger Church." *Man, urban Vancouver*

Some parishioners in urban Vancouver prefer the *Book of Common Prayer* and some, the *Book of Alternative Services*; most feel that their church community is able to support the use of both at alternating services. The *BCP* is preferred by more of those claiming to come from church communities with aging populations: "People in our church community don't like change."

Music in the church is also a common topic of discussion. For some, particularly in evangelical church communities, the inclusion of music that may be outside the parameters of "approved" music is discussed often, as is the inclusion of dance. Among these church communities, the issue of music and the relevance of the Anglican Church of Canada are often intertwined.

> "Our (local) spiritual leaders know what is appropriate and right for our congregation; they shouldn't have to talk to anyone about what music we will include. They should be in control of these things. They know our community and what will reach our souls. This doesn't need to be decided by some hierarchy, by people who are not part of our community. I think that the Anglican Church of Canada is out of touch with what people want from their in-church experience." *Woman, Vancouver, Anglican evangelical church community*

Even among church communities outside the evangelical movement, some are concerned that the music of the church isn't interesting or relevant any longer.

> "Well, in Victorian times I suspect that the Anglican Church was really 'current'; now it all seems so old-fashioned. I think that we need to really update our tunes." *Man, urban Vancouver*

Issue: *Changing nature of the church community population*

The changing nature of the population of individual church communities, including concerns about aging populations, declining number of youth involved in the church community, and emerging immigrant influence on previously mono-cultural populations, causes some concern.

Some participants from established downtown Vancouver church communities feel that attendance and participation is, by its nature, are cyclical. Some feel that it is to be expected that older people will dominate and that their "rights" in the community should take precedence over "newcomers." They would argue that this will "sort itself out" as more and more Baby Boomers return to the Church as they grow older.

Some evangelical church parishioners from both downtown and suburban Vancouver feel that attendance and participation in their own church community is actually growing, in some cases substantially. These parishioners feel that this is happening because their church community is an integrated part of the lives of those who are involved. Furthermore, they feel that their church community is at the core of the daily lives of its members, and that membership in this special community is, of itself, important and relevant.

Some feel that what it means to be Anglican is tied too tightly to "rules" that may no longer be interesting or relevant to those who are seeking a better grasp of their own spirituality. These participants are the most likely to feel that any decline in membership experienced by the Anglican Church of Canada may be "growing the ranks of other churches," rather than indicating cyclical church attendance or overall decline in participation in communities of faith. They point to alternative religions, those outside the mainstream, as the fastest growing, and they wonder why it is that they seem to have greater appeal.

Others argue that the Church is not in the entertainment business, and that if "this is the sort of experience that people want to have, then, well ... they are just not Anglican."

A few argue that what is lacking is clear vision and direction from the leaders of the Anglican Church of Canada. What is the vision for the future of the Church? What commitment will the Church make to being alert, sensitive, mindful, and active in a meaningful way to a diverse population? How will the Church reconcile the different needs of these diverse and multicultural church communities? Multicultural communities are more likely to include family members across a broad spectrum of age. How will these communities be truly integrated with the Anglican Church of Canada?

Issue: *Referendum — treaty rights, lands, and settlements*

The BC government released copies of the *Referendum on Principles for Treaty Negotiations*, dealing with treaty rights, lands, and settlements, the week before the discussion groups in British Columbia. The referendum was the top-of-mind and overriding issue among those living in downtown Vancouver parishes.

The major concern is that the BC government is asking those living in the province to vote on an issue when many feel ill-informed. The results of the referendum will, by law, be binding.

The Anglican bishops of the Province of British Columbia have made a statement of position on this issue, which was published as a "paid announcement" in local Vancouver newspapers. Many of those from downtown Vancouver churches feel that the bishops' statement is good and appropriate, as it clearly allows everyone to know where the Church stands on this important issue.

Some claim to be a bit uncomfortable with the bishops taking such a public stand. Some are concerned, because press reports have suggested that the Anglican Church is telling people how they must vote.

> "We are Anglicans, not Catholics; we don't need to be told how to think, we know how to think." *Man, lifelong Anglican, urban Vancouver*

Others argue that the bishops have made it very clear that that this vote is an individual decision and that the Anglican Church does not "tell anyone" how to vote.

> "Taking a stand like this, well, it makes me proud to be part of the Anglican Church. I think that the Church should be taking more of a stand on many issues." *Woman, lifelong Anglican, urban Vancouver*

While not everyone agrees with the position taken by the bishops, there is an overall sense of pride that the bishops have clearly stated an opinion.

Issue: *The Anglican Church as a social advocate*

Most urban Vancouver participants feel that it was more important than ever that the Anglican Church of Canada, the dioceses and the parishes, all act as social advocates at a national level, and within their own communities. Many said that, with cuts in social spending, there has also been a decrease in those who are prepared, willing, or paid to take a social advocacy position. They feel that the Church must be willing to take on more of the responsibility of advocacy.

> "The most vulnerable and least able to defend themselves are the ones most affected by cuts in social spending. Our church community is sometimes the only place where people can find help." *Woman, five years in the Anglican Church, from a Catholic Church tradition, urban Vancouver*

As in Toronto, parishioners in urban Vancouver were very concerned about government cutbacks, particularly in social services, education, and medical care. The lack of secular support for social services from the City of Vancouver and from the Government of British Columbia is creating a greater demand for church communities to provide physical and emotional help to those outside the church. This is putting increased pressure on those already hard at work on behalf of their own church communities.

Issue: *Integrating new members of the community into the volunteer needs of the Church*

While all of those who participate in church communities in urban Vancouver said that their communities are warm and welcoming, it is clear that this is in fact not completely true. In some congregations, membership rarely involves the entry of "new people." Their neighbourhoods are established; those who attend and participate are people who have always participated in that particular community. While these church communities would certainly make an "outsider" feel like an honoured guest, they have little, if any, experience with people "moving into the neighbourhood."

> "I think that it is a difficult matter. Going to and participating in a community of faith gives me a feeling and sense of comfort. I am part of that community; if I were not around, they would notice. Maybe because we are a community, we don't reach out to strangers as we should, to make them feel welcome; maybe we are too tight knit ... I don't know, but I do wonder if perhaps that is why we don't grow as other church communities say that they are doing." *Man, urban Vancouver*

Those who have more recently moved to the Vancouver area are often discomfited by how difficult it is to feel that they have an active part to play in their new church community. For some, it takes moving from one congregation to another to find a "home church." Most of the discomfort comes from a sense of exclusion from roles in the new church that they had previously enjoyed before their move.

> "When I came to Vancouver, I really wanted to go to the Cathedral. It is such a beautiful, beautiful building. People were friendly enough when I went to church. There was always someone with a smile and a greeting, but over and over again I asked to be directed to things that I might do as a volunteer, and I just didn't get any response. So I asked about the Vestry committee, as that is what I had done in my old church. I was told that the committee had been doing the job for years, and that they didn't need anybody new; so I asked about other things, and was told, 'Dear, if we need you, we will let you know.' Well, I went 'shopping,' and I found a dear little church not far from where I live. They needed and wanted me. I just love it there." *Woman, urban Vancouver*

3.2.2 Vancouver: Suburban Parishes

While many of the key concerns were similar to those of their urban counterparts, representatives of churches from suburban Vancouver placed significantly different emphasis on these issues.

The key areas of concern among those from suburban Vancouver churches included the relationship of the local church to the Anglican Church of Canada, the changing population of their own church communities, the referendum, and diversity of styles of worship.

Issue: *The local church versus the Anglican Church of Canada*

The question of autonomy from the Anglican Church was at the top of the issues under discussion among suburban Vancouver church communities. The issue of autonomy includes three key issue areas: the economic impact of the residential schools litigation, diversity of worship, and changes in population, including immigrants moving into church communities that until recently have been predominately white, older, and lifelong Anglican.

> "We have talked about our ability to survive if the Anglican Church of Canada is bankrupted by the lawsuits of the Indigenous peoples. We are a growing evangelical church community. We are building a

new church because we have outgrown our old meeting area. We talk about breaking away from the Anglican Church of Canada and being independent, autonomous … because we don't all feel that the Anglican Church of Canada is of much value to us. We have a bit different form of worship than most. Many of our congregation come from non-Christian cultures, we have all ages in our church, but we are 99 per cent Chinese. What have we in common with the Anglican Church of Canada, we ask? And the answer is always, not much at all. I think what keeps us in the Anglican Church for now is that some of us come from an Anglican mission tradition, and we see ourselves as continuing that tradition with our mission-style church here in Canada. This style of worship may be different from many traditional Anglican churches in Canada, but the Anglican mission tradition is our traditional church." *Man, suburban Vancouver, evangelical Chinese*

> "We are a small church, our community is really farther away than would be considered a suburb. We just worry about keeping afloat." *Woman, suburban Vancouver*

> "In our church community we are Anglicans, and we will stay Anglicans, but most people don't even see themselves as part of the diocese, much less the Anglican Church of Canada." *Man, suburban Vancouver, traditional*

Issue: *The changing population of church communities*

Some churches in suburban Vancouver worry that they are not placing enough emphasis on programs for youth. They worry that their church community is declining because of the advancing age of church members.

> "If we don't get some young people into our church, we won't survive long. You need young people to keep the money rolling in." *Woman, suburban Vancouver*

At the same time, some parishioners in suburban churches that are traditional in nature are having difficulties welcoming new church members from other backgrounds or traditions, and are concerned about the changes that might follow such shifts in the population of their congregations.

"I don't know where it will go. We are mostly an older congregation, but the neighbourhood has changed, and now we seem to be getting a lot of foreigners. They seem to want different things than we do. Sometimes it doesn't seem all that happy around our church." *Man, suburban Vancouver*

"Racial issues exist in churches, particularly in the suburbs, I find. I was a member of a parish at University that had great diversity. My wife's a Japanese-Canadian, a visible minority, and there she didn't really stand out. I don't consider myself white, as I have Korean and Ukrainian and French and Scottish blood in me. When we started to look for a church out here, we knew right away when we were not welcome. That isn't right for a church." *Man, suburban Vancouver*

Issue: *The diversity of styles of worship*

The issue of diversity includes the changing needs of the local church community as well as the changing nature of these communities. Most feel that changes made to embrace diversity were made at a local level to address the needs of local community members, rather than as part of the vision for the future of the Anglican Church of Canada. Indeed, the bigger Church didn't play a very big role in the eyes of the parishioners in suburban Vancouver.

"Maybe to have a thriving community, it is necessary to do something completely different. We are surprised at the success of our Thursday service. When we first got to the church, my dad was afraid that he was going to have to shut it down. But now we have families and maybe 30 or so people on Thursdays, and more people coming on Sundays. I hear people say it is because my dad finds a way to give something for everybody. Maybe that is what other churches should do too." *Young adult daughter of a parish priest, suburban Vancouver, evangelical*

"It seems to me that, at our church, we are trying to cultivate something that is personal to the community where we live. It isn't necessarily exactly like other Anglican churches, but even so, I don't really hear any talk about moving away from the Anglican Church. Most of our members are long-time Anglicans — it is part of their identity. I guess what I think is that the Church can keep some things the same and change some to greet the times. I think we do that in our church community. *Woman, suburban Vancouver*

While change from the *BCP* to the *BAS* and the addition of new hymn books has created some controversy in some church communities, most feel that the need for diverse forms of worship has been met in their church by offering a variety of services using different forms.

"Our style of service is traditional to most Anglican evangelical churches, I think. We use the *BAS*, but we have our own music whenever we want something a bit different. We even have a band that plays sometimes, although it is really supposed to be for celebration, rather than every day." *Man, suburban Vancouver; evangelical*

"In my church we have everything: the old prayer book, the old songs, and all the new stuff. Different services use different material, that's all. No one minds; you just learn which service you like better and you go to that one. It works out just fine." *Woman, suburban Vancouver*

"We fought, and finally won in our church, for inclusive language." *Woman, suburban Vancouver*

"My dad and I were just talking about this the other day. We both agree that the Church has to be careful that the entertainment value of the service doesn't get in the way of worship. We have all ages in our church, because it is part of the Chinese tradition to do things together as a family. I don't know where I will end up when I finish university and leave my parents' home to have a home of my own. I will hope that it keeps in mind the importance of worship, that it has meaningful and fun programs for young people outside of the usual worship times. That is the sort of church that I will be looking to find." *Young Chinese-Canadian man, suburban Vancouver*

Issue: *The BC referendum — treaty rights, lands, and settlements*

In the suburban church communities represented at these meetings, the participants were, without regard to their usual political position, confused, even angry, over the BC referendum. As with their urban counterparts, the biggest concern is that the referendum vote will be binding on the BC government. Most feel that they don't have enough information to make an informed decision.

> "Have you seen the referendum? It would be a joke if it weren't so scary. I have done quite a lot of reading on Aboriginal rights, but I can't even begin to answer the questions." *Man, suburban Vancouver*

Many feel that it was important for the bishops to take a stand on the referendum questions, even if they decided later to vote in a different manner than outlined by the bishops' comments. The thinking is that if the Church is willing to take a stand, then the issue must be important. Some feel that this would "get more people thinking and talking about it, at least."

> "I felt proud and glad when the bishop wrote that letter. I don't feel that he was telling us how to vote, but rather saying what he thinks. I feel that it is important for our church to take a stand on these issues." *Woman, suburban Vancouver*

Issue: *Cutbacks in social services, a decline in social justice*

Some of the participants' concerns were very personal and related directly to their own communities or their personal concerns about economic stability. Some are very concerned about economic security in their own communities. Many feel vulnerable because of government cutbacks.

> "This government is very liberal; they want to get rid of things and change things, and our town is mostly people who work in the civil services; many people are afraid for their jobs." *Woman, suburban Vancouver*

> "Our area is supposed to be affluent, but you see real street people, not just in downtown Vancouver anymore, but out here too. It is wrong with so many people homeless, particularly families." *Man, suburban Vancouver*

Others feel a keen sense of responsibility for those who need help in their community. Many church communities are feeling pressure as new changes, restructuring, and cutbacks to programs are announced.

"Our church tries to help with clothes and food and so on for people less fortunate in our area, but there is so much to be done; we don't think that we are helping enough. The trouble is that there aren't enough volunteers for our programs. Some people are willing; others would just rather stay out of it. Some of us think that the church should take a stronger stand about social justice, so that people could hear from the church about their responsibilities to their communities. We learned about it in our churches in our day. Why don't they talk about it much these days? Things are much worse now, I think, than they were when I was a girl." *Woman, suburban Vancouver*

Issue: *Homosexuality — blessing of same-sex unions*

All participants reported that, within their own church communities, the issue of homosexuality, and specifically the blessing of same-sex unions, has been a hotly debated topic. In some instances, participants reported that this has been a divisive issue. In others, talking openly about the topic has created a calmer and more tolerant environment.

The "issue" or concern of church communities in suburban Vancouver centres on the blessing of same-sex unions, and generally not on the larger issues expressed in urban Vancouver related to full inclusion of gay and lesbian members into the active life of that community. There was little mention of ordination or of participation in sacraments.

Most church communities, we were told, intend to be tolerant, but a few admit that tolerance for homosexuality is low among those in their congregation, and that gay and lesbian persons, while not rejected, would certainly not feel that they were included as full participants in their community. In these few churches, for some the issue is morality, but for others the issue is fear and, perhaps, just inexperience.

"Our diocese had dialogues within the parish, and they had different parishes pair up. The discussion was about what a same-sex blessing would look like, and what it would mean. We weren't very clear on the issues. Our group ended up feeling that it should be a fairly general blessing, but that there should definitely be one. It seemed just wrong to deny it after we had talked about it. We had a good facilitator who didn't let things get out of hand." *Man, suburban Vancouver*

"We too had a twinning with another parish; it was very confrontational and very upsetting to everybody." *Woman, suburban Vancouver*

3.3.1 Red Deer Parishes

One group of parishioners participated in a discussion session in Red Deer. These participants came from church communities in Red Deer and from other parishes as far away as LaDuc, Alberta. The parish communities represented included "small urban," "suburban Red Deer," and rural parishes.

Participants in the Red Deer discussion explained that the people in their area are more interested in what happens locally than in national or international issues. For example, settlement of litigation related to residential schools is a concern, but only in terms of how it might impact on their own local church.

Changes in the Church and the role of the Church as a resource to parishes, discussions in church communities about continued support for the Anglican Church of Canada and the survival of the Anglican Church of Canada, the decreasing population in the Anglican Church of Canada, leadership in church communities, long tenure on executive committees, and fewer volunteers at the local level were the most commonly mentioned issues among those from Red Deer and the surrounding area.

Issue: *Changes in the Church and the role of the Church as a resource to parishes*

The issue of changes in the Church has more to do with the role played by the Anglican Church of Canada and the diocese on behalf of the parish church than with liturgy or theology. Many wonder, "What are we getting for our money?" Some feel that the visibility, and even the accountability, of the Anglican Church of Canada is questioned in their local church community.

> "In our church, I hear two different questions over and over again. One is, 'What are we getting for our money?' And the other is more along the lines of, 'I'd like to feel pride; I'd like to be able to say, "we" do this and that.' People in our church talk about it. 'If we give them this money, what will happen to it?' And, 'What's the benefit to us?'" *Man, Red Deer*

Some church communities have already decided that their intent is to leave the Anglican Church. Some have already incorporated, and many are looking at the legal implications of "separation."

Some church communities would have "stayed put" forever, if their ownership of the church building were not threatened. In these parishes, the building is as much a part of the community's definition of itself as are the individual members who share the long history of the community.

> "I have always been an Anglican, for my whole life. I must say that, in our church, we talk about this distance between the parish and the bigger Church, and we have just about decided that we don't need the hassle. We want to be sure that we are the ones who own our own church building, and we think we do; after that, well, we may just decide to go it on our own. We don't need the added expense of all the lawsuits. What do they have to do with us?" *Woman, Red Deer*

> "I have to say that I'm disappointed with the big Church. I know this is personal, but it is a good example of what I mean, I think. I sent an e-mail some time ago in connection with a cell group ministry for the national Church, and I said, 'This is what we're doing in our parish and I would appreciate any type of resource or information you could give me.' I waited for three days for a response ... three days by e-mail! In their response, they just sort of blew me off. No, we don't have anything; you might try your diocese. I thought, yes, well, I'm not surprised. I expect the national Church or dioceses or whatever will assist the parish, and sadly, I don't think that happens much anymore." *Woman, Red Deer*

Some feel that there has been a drastic decline in participation by the Anglican Church of Canada in other places around the world. Mission activity in Third World countries is seen by many as an important part of being Anglican and an important role for the Church.

Some reported that giving money to "overseas missions" as a child was one clear thing that they knew about the Anglican Church of Canada. Now some wonder, do these sorts of missions still exist?

> "I have been thinking about this quite a lot lately. When I went looking for what the Anglican Church is doing in the Third World, particularly in Afghanistan, it doesn't seem to me that the Church is doing very much. I have always thought that we raised money for this sort of thing. I'm surprised that I don't find very much. Helping others in faraway lands has always seemed right and important to me. Why has this changed?" *Woman, Red Deer*

Issue: *Decreasing population in the Anglican Church of Canada*

A few of the church communities represented indicated that the population of their own local church is aging. Some feel that there are fewer young families, children, and teens participating in the services at their churches.

However, many feel that perhaps "it is different" in Alberta; the economy is growing and people are moving to Alberta from other places. Most said that they feel that their own local church populations are growing and that programs and activities for young people are on the rise.

> "We're naturally growing, if for no other reason than our town is growing. Two years ago, we didn't have a Sunday school; now we have about 15 or so kids on a Sunday. I think it is natural and right that teenagers don't come as often. I didn't go to church when I was a teenager. They have other things to do at this stage of their life. At our church at the moment, I would have to say that 80 per cent of our church population is over 55. But we don't worry that much; the younger people will be back with their own families soon. They will be back when they have families of their own, or they will be like us — they will come back a second time after their families have grown and gone. This is just the way that people are." *Woman, Red Deer*

> "In our church community we have a strong core group. Our attendance numbers go up and down, but the core of us keep things going. We have the same number of people on our rolls as we did a few years ago, and we have added some new ones, who have moved here from the Maritimes. We have a few families with babies, people in the middle, and old people; it is the same as it has always been. I think people worry about nothing … or maybe it is true that things are different in Alberta." *Man, Red Deer*

Issue: *Where are the people who are 30 to 40 years old?*

A few worry that the Anglican Church doesn't have as much appeal as other church denominations.

> "It is boring to be an Anglican. We don't know how to have much fun." *Man, Red Deer*

> "I was just talking to my dad about this the other day. He said, 'The

> Anglican Church isn't an easy place to find Christ, but it is a good place to grow in Christ.'" *Man, Red Deer*

Some indicated that their own church communities are actively seeking ways of marketing to adults in their 30s and 40s — ways to make it interesting and engaging for all members of a family.

> "Part of the problem is that older people don't like change and younger people don't like things to stay the same as they have always been. I think that we are losing some families to other churches that are more fun or where there are more activities." *Woman, Red Deer*

> "Well, we have been creating some new ways of doing things. It isn't much fun for people in their 30s and 40s to be an Anglican. We have found that our cell ministry is revitalizing the interests of people in this age category. In our church community, we think it is our job to make the church community an interesting place. We don't believe that there is a place in our worship service for all of the new Christian music, for example, but we love it as a way to just celebrate our connection to Christianity." *Woman, Red Deer*

A few worried about new evangelical churches. The appeal of these new churches is the "entertainment value," they feel. Some worry that the Anglican Church is at a real disadvantage.

> "I do worry about the new churches in our area. One is getting over a thousand people a week! I know that some of our Anglicans are going there instead of to our church. Some of them are going there because their kids show an interest in the music and the general sense of community. The Anglican Church just isn't there for these young people, and that is too bad." *Man, Red Deer*

Most participants in this discussion do not feel that their own churches were at risk from declining populations.

A decreasing population in the Anglican Church of Canada worries some, because they feel that the more vital church parishes of Alberta will have to "pay for" the old and dying parishes.

Some do worry that the music and the family atmosphere of some of the "new churches" in the area may attract more young people, and through them, their families. Some may be moving away from the Anglican tradition to join these new communities.

"My daughter sings in a choir at the Pentecostal church. We have been there a couple of times; so I know a bit about what they do there. They sing and they have a lot of fun. They have very little liturgy. They have very little of what I call 'church.' But they do have a lot of people." *Woman, Red Deer*

"We've been to the Alliance Church, because our granddaughter sings in a junior choir that has over 65 members from grades 1 to 5. Sixty-five members in a junior choir! And they have wonderful music and they have a great preacher, and I could sit and listen to him for hours. You could sit there, and everybody has their Bibles and listens to him. I think it is church, just more joyful than ours. I don't think that is altogether a bad thing." *Man, Red Deer*

Issues: *Leadership and direction in church communities*
Self-directed leadership
The effect of executive committees that stay on "too long"

A number of concerns were raised related to leadership at the parish and diocesan level, both among priests and bishops, and among lay leaders.

There is concern that the Anglican Church of Canada needs to do a "better job" of recruiting priests, as some feel that there is an urgent need for younger priests, particularly males.

"Oh, I think that there are probably enough priests around, but have you noticed that most of them are old, and that most of the new ones are women? It may be different in different places, I don't know about that, but in our church community that isn't what most of us feel is needed here." *Woman, Red Deer*

Communication between diocesan and parish levels is seen as lacking by some, as is a sense of vision and leadership coming from the local bishops.

"With a bishop we had a while back, we would hear from him; we got material from the diocese office telling us about his vision, and so on. With this bishop, I don't remember ever seeing anything about vision. We expect some meaningful leadership from our church higher-ups." *Woman, Red Deer*

Some find that lay leadership has rested in the hands of a few members of the parish, resulting in stagnation, and yet again, a loss of leadership and the potential for vision. Others have responded to the lack of leadership they experience by finding ways to take on roles and responsibilities at a local level and create their own vision.

> "We have had the same people on our executive committee for 20 years. They do the same things year after year, and make the same decisions. Nothing changes. When we have tried to talk about getting different people onto the executive, we are just told that 'our time will come.' Well, I'm 52 years old. When will that time be?" *Man, Red Deer*

> "Well, I'm not sure if we are great leaders, but we decided that a cell group ministry was appropriate in our church community. So we started with the intention that we would get together some people, and we dealt with couples, we taught ourselves how to be facilitators, so that we could go to other parishes and start cell groups there too. We've got a fantastic cell group, and we have enthusiasm with what's going on in our local church and in the world. We work on understanding what good Christian people do and should do, and what the Christian response should be, and it just generates some great discussion. We look forward to our time together. Although it wasn't our intent, what we have found is that we no longer care very much about vision or leadership from outside sources in the Church. We have it with each other." *Red Deer, couple*

Issues: *Fewer volunteers available for local church activities and needs*
More to do, less people to help

Cutbacks to government-supported programs have created a greater need for volunteers and fundraising in local communities. Many people find that they are volunteering on both a community level and with their church. There is simply too much to do, and too little in the way of human resources to get it done.

Some feel that the problem is not with the number of volunteers but with the manner in which volunteer help is employed. Models for successful volunteering and fundraising are available in most communities. Church communities need to look to these success stories and find a way to incorporate these models into their church community's activities.

> "A problem we face in our town and in our church community — it is always the same people doing the volunteer things over and over again. It is hard to get new people to come in, because we all know

what to do and how to do things, and others don't know how we do things, and they might want to do things differently ... sometimes it is frustrating. Our town is pretty small, so we don't have much new blood. The thing is that people who have never volunteered before always seem to want to start out with top jobs. That isn't the way that we do things. They should know that you have to work your way up. Those of us who are in the know will let them know when they are ready. That is just the way it works." *Man, Red Deer*

"I feel a bit differently about volunteers, maybe because I am with the Rotary, which is a great organization. I think that we could have plenty of volunteers in our church community if we had better goals, and if we would approach it more like a business. People like to know that they are part of something, and lots of people understand that best by having a job to do, one where they are accountable for a job getting done. Well, we have started to use this approach in our church. Everybody, no matter what their talents, is expected to pitch in. We haven't always done it this way. In the past there was just a tight little club of people who complained all the time that they had too much to do. I know, because I used to be one of them. But, back to the Rotary, once I had seen how it worked there, I took it back to my church. It has made a wonderful difference for us all." *Man, Red Deer*

Issue: *Church liturgy*

While there is still ongoing discussion about the *BCP* versus the *BAS*, many churches have found a way to satisfy most parishioners. Some use one book exclusively, and some alternate books between services.

Many church communities are discussing music. Music was mentioned by many as one aspect of worship that brings them "joy." Some are worried about defining what is appropriate music for worship, and which music should be reserved for celebrations outside of times of worship. There is a feeling among some that there is a liturgical "reason" for music that is intended for worship, which should be used in praise.

Some feel that the music of the Anglican Church is one of its traditional, defining features, and that it should therefore only be used in that context and in the manner that it has "always" been used.

"We still have some people talking about the *Book of Common Prayer* versus the *Book of Alternative Services*. We use both, at different services, but this isn't possible at some of our neighbour churches, where they only have one service on Sunday, or services alternate from one church to the other. Personally, I think we should stop talking about it, use the *Book of Alternative Services*, and maybe focus on getting the music up to date. Other churches in our area have fine music that people really enjoy. Why is it not the Anglican thing to have newer music? I just don't understand the thinking. We lose our young people to places where they can get involved with the music. I've heard people say that the Anglican church people all take things too seriously, and that other churches don't have the same class. Well, I ask you this, if the music isn't relevant to the people who hear it, how can it be the music of the Lord?" *Man, Red Deer*

Issue: *Building a church — fundraising*

Some church communities are facing special issues that cause them concern. A few are concerned about the "competition" and about their own fundraising efforts.

"It used to be that the Church was at the centre of our whole community. Now, with government cutbacks and so on, there is fundraising for everything — the school, the parks, programs for kids. People only want to give so much. We do fundraisers that are fun, so that people will feel that they are getting something for their money. This is different than when the fundraisers were part of our social life. This is business, and it is hard work. I'm not sure how much more we can raise for our church building. It is a worry." *Woman, Red Deer*

Issue: *In from the Cold program*

Cutbacks in social services and changes in employment opportunities are thought by some in Red Deer to demand a greater need for involvement from church communities.

"We are very proud of our In from the Cold program. We have nearly doubled our volume in the past year. We are proud because we have been able to cope with the added need that this represents, but we are worried too. The need keeps growing, and we don't know if we will be able to grow our capacity. There is something very wrong with the social system when so many people have to reach out for help." *Woman, Red Deer*

3.4.1 St. John's: Rural Parishioners

Concerns about declining church populations, people leaving the church community to join other churches or who are just "falling away," the aging population of the area, and the lack of involvement among young people in the Church are all shared concerns among parishioners who attend rural churches just outside St. John's. Many are also worried about the lack of funds to keep churches open and maintained. The number and frequency of fundraising efforts that are stretching the limits of those who might contribute is also a cause for concern and anxiety

Issue: *Declining church populations*

The decline in the populations of local congregations is a concern to many. Some express concern that the Church has aging congregations, with few or no younger members. Without younger people, there is concern that the economic well will dry up and the Church will die along with the aging parishioners.

> "I think our numbers have been about the same for the past five years or so. The trouble is that it is the same people and they/we are getting older. Many of us don't have much spare money; some of us are retired and have a small fixed income. If we don't have young people in our church, where will the money come from? Who will be there to do the work that must be done?" *Man, rural parish*

Others suggested that the problem is not so much that the young people are not joining, as it is that they are leaving Newfoundland altogether. These parishioners see the problem of migration from the province as the source of the Church's population decline.

> "I think that everywhere in Newfoundland, the problem isn't aging and the like, it is that all of our young talented people are leaving home to go into St. John's or off island. They are going away to find work in other places. Out-migration will be the death of Newfoundland, not just our churches." *Woman, rural parish*

Still others wonder if there is something lacking in their own church that is resulting in the decline. They worry that divisions in the Church over liturgy, and form and style of worship may be turning away people who are seeking a spiritual experience. Others suggested that a greater sense of leadership, energy, and vision from the clergy might help to rejuvenate their congregations.

"I'm sure that the other churches have their little in-fighting too, but I wish that, in our church, there were less conversation about using this book or that book, and more talk about spirituality. I don't know if the reason people leave our church is because they like the entertainment better at other churches or because they have a spiritual hunger that we just don't fill. I sometimes feel that way myself." *Man, rural parish*

"We don't get the best priests out here. Mostly we get the old ones, or the ones just starting out. Either way, we don't seem to get the real good ones. Maybe if we had one of the ones with more energy or experience we would do better? Maybe then we could have some leadership and vision from them. I know we talk about this in our church. None of us would go and talk to them about personal matters, as we used to do in the old days." *Woman, rural parish*

Issue: *We need younger people in our church*

Declining membership in Anglican churches is thought, by some, to be about the specific nature of the church service. In considering this issue, many try to think about what "the competition" is doing right. The concern about the lack of youth in the Church is often not about how the Church might better serve or be of more interest to youth, but rather that if youth are not brought into the Church today, then in the future, the Church may cease to have an economic base. Being of interest to youth becomes the "bargaining chip," part of the "marketing plan."

"When we look around our church, most of the heads are either grey or bald-headed. This doesn't make me feel that there is much of a future for the place if we don't get some new people pretty soon. We talk lots about how to get young people interested, but we are all over the hill. How can we know what might be right for young people? We don't even know who we might talk to about it. I confess, we feel a bit lost." *Man, rural parish*

Issue: *Too many fundraising activities*

Some of the rural churches represented have fundraising events throughout the year. Others rely on one or two major events. The concern was much the same among all those represented. They reported that the total number of fundraising events in their local community has grown as budgets for schools and other local institutions have been cut back.

This means that there is increased pressure for individuals to donate funds to many more organizations than in the past. This combination of fundraising activities makes it ever more difficult to raise the money that is needed to maintain their church properties or to support church activities.

Some are also concerned that the nature of fundraising has changed. For many, working on a fundraising event or attending one was, in the past, a time of fellowship. Some feel that fellowship is no longer part of the fundraising activity.

> "It sometimes gets hard to think up something new to do to raise money. We've tried them all at our church. We have suppers, car washes; we have 'slave days' and dances. It seems to me that we make less and less at our fundraisers; so we have to have another one. There aren't that many of us to run these events; so we are wearing down. And, just when we think we are getting ahead, we get hit with a letter from the bishop needing us to raise some more money. People in our area are beginning to feel tapped out." *Man, rural parish*

> "Fundraising is just out of hand at our church. There is something going on every month, something to raise more money for this and for that. I used to like all the activities; when we were a young family, just about our whole social life was centred around the church 'doings,' but now it doesn't feel so much like fellowship, but more like a business. I think that we have gone too far with this. I miss the fellowship." *Woman, rural parish*

3.4.2 St. John's: Urban and Suburban Parishes

Community outreach programs, keeping young people in the church community, and appropriate forms of worship were shared concerns among parishioners in both urban and suburban parishes in St. John's.

Issue: *Outreach — responsibility to the larger community*

Outreach programs are important to parishioners in St John's. Wanting to be helpful to those in their own community who "fall on bad times" is a shared vision. The issue is that the number of people who need help, and the types of help needed, seem to be expanding. Some wonder if their church community will be able to meet the demand. They also wonder why the need is growing so fast.

> "We don't have a lot of money here in Newfoundland. We are seeing more and more people in need of shelter and food — not

through any fault of their own. We have an active outreach program in our church, we try to do what we can to help. But it just keeps growing and growing. It is a worry; we are stretched for people and money to help." *Woman, urban St. John's*

"We have food drives to fill our food bank. We are on the phones all the time looking for affordable housing for a family down on their luck. Everybody who is able helps out with this in our church, but we just don't have enough people to do the job. We worry, because if we don't do it, who will? We are honestly worn down, and some of us are very worried. We can't push our own church members to give more money because they don't have any more money. We are not a rich group of people." *Man, urban St. John's*

"Speaking of outreach, what ever happened to those missions that we used to hear about in faraway places? I always thought those were the best lessons. We learned about other places, and we also could feel that we were doing some real good." *Woman, urban St. John's*

Issue: *We need more young people in our church*

Developing programs to attract and keep youth in their congregations is also a much-talked about goal in many St. John's churches. But the motives for wanting youth are questioned by some. For some, involving youth in the Church is a matter of economic necessity; without new members to take over the responsibility for maintenance of the Church, the Church may wither and die.

"Well, we have talked about getting a youth leader who would work to attract young people, particularly pre-teens and teens, to come to our church. We think that if we could get the kids to come, their parents might follow. It seems to work in the other churches in town. We wonder, though, if there are enough of those sorts of programs already going. We don't know for sure that it would work, and it could be expensive to run." *Man, urban St. John's*

"You have to have young people in your church, or when we all die off there won't be anybody to keep things going financially. Other churches do it; we have to find a way to be interesting to young people, or be willing to just 'shut the doors.' I think the Anglican Church has a lot to offer, but we are not doing enough that is relevant to young people." *Man, urban St. John's*

> "Our church is more evangelical than some of the others here tonight. We are growing so fast that we don't have room for people anymore. Maybe other churches should take a look at what we do. We have young people and old people, new people all the time coming from other churches. We have a youth worker and we have outreach programs too. We are Anglicans, but nobody calls us boring." *Man, urban St. John's*

As in other regions, some feel that the lack of attendance of youth is a matter of life cycles, and that they will return to the Church once they are older.

> "We get young people when they are little. They come with their parents. We have a small Sunday school, really babysitting for the little ones. But once they are about ten they are off doing other things on a Sunday. Maybe that is the problem — there is no longer a family day. We have talked about getting a youth co-ordinator to develop some things for us. But really, all that we do is talk. I think that most people in our church figure that these kids today will come back when they have families of their own." *Woman, urban St. John's*

Issue: *"Appropriate" forms of Anglican worship*

There is real debate among various church communities about what is "appropriate" Anglican Church worship, and where it might cross the line into entertainment, or even "some other kind of religion."

Participants in the urban St. John's discussion came from churches that they described as "very old traditional Anglican" to "a lively evangelical church community." It is clear that the differences in forms of worship are openly, even hotly, debated.

Some participants feel that there is room within the Anglican Church to support different forms of worship. Some feel that the leadership of the Church should give better guidance related to the forms of worship that are considered appropriate. Some feel that a particular form of worship defines a "true Anglican" and that this should not, and cannot, be debated.

> "I don't believe that the Anglican Church should be about competition and about entertainment. I think that is what the more evangelical churches are doing. I don't see anything wrong with singing up-beat music, but it isn't church, it is entertainment. We stick to

the old *Book of Common Prayer*, and we are proud to be very conservative and traditional. We feel that it is important to preserve tradition. If other people want to worship in others ways, that's fine, but it is *not* Anglican." *Man, urban St. John's*

"Well, in our church we have different types of services at different times, some short, some long. Maybe it goes with the size of the church? I myself like a service with communion every week. When we go down to visit my sister, they only have a service at their church every other week now, because they share a priest with another church. They only have one service, and it has communion. We use the *BAS* at our main service, but I would personally like to see them use (the) *BCP* more often." *Woman, urban St. John's*

"We are a neighbourhood church and we do have families and some young people, but we have noticed lately that we are losing some of our people to other churches, particularly the Pentecostal church, where they have fun programs for young children and teens. We have enough kids in our church for an active Sunday school, but not enough for a youth choir. And anyway, the music we sing just isn't fun for kids. It worries me and it confuses me. I love the way it feels to be part of our church service. I get comfort from knowing what is going to happen next each time. It makes me feel safe, but what about young people? Maybe the Church as we know it is old-fashioned and uptight, like my granddaughter says. She likes to sing at her church, and she says that she feels joy with that. I feel joy when I hear them sing. I don't see how that can be wrong, but it doesn't feel like church to me." *Woman, suburban St. John's*

(In response to the comment above) "Now, isn't that just the thing, I think that my quiet little church is the Anglican Church, and those with a different sort of worship think that they are the Anglican Church. Where is our leadership on this? Both can't be the 'right way' to be Anglican, can it? This isn't the old 'high church and low church' argument. This is something different altogether. I understand the evangelical church approach, for, say, our overseas missions. They have a different set of problems. But aren't Anglicans more traditional? I don't want to see the Church lose its traditions." *Man, urban St. John's*

4.0 CONCERNS OF THE CLERGY

Discussions were held in Toronto, Ontario; Red Deer, Alberta; Vancouver, British Columbia; and in St. John's, Newfoundland. In each community, a group of clergy was invited to attend a "coffee chat." These discussions were informal. Some were conducted as workshops and others in a discussion format.

Participants ranged from those new to the clergy to those who are now retired. Some came from large urban church communities, some from suburban churches, and still others from "two point" rural churches.[4]

4.1 Key Issues for Clergy: A Snapshot across Canada — April/May 2002

The following is an overview of the clergy's view of the issues talked about within the Church. These issues include both concerns that are felt to be important within their own parish and others that they say are important to themselves and to other clergy within the Anglican Church.

While many of the concerns and issues raised among the clergy were shared in common, there were clear regional differences in the interpretation of those issues. These differences are also noted.

Issue: *Survival of local church communities*

Financial concerns are causing anxiety in many church communities. The concerns range from immediate needs, such as fixing a leaking roof, to real concerns about the ability of the Anglican Church of Canada to survive the settlement of the residential schools litigation.

Some church communities are concerned about their immediate survival. With declining and aging membership, some are looking for new opportunities to grow their ranks. Others are more concerned about losing their church building "as an asset of the Church." Some feel that their church community is worth more to the Church if the community is closed or amalgamated with another, than if it is limping along in need of subsidy. Clergy told us that this is frustrating and troubling to older congregations who don't want to have to change their patterns or move to another church. Many worry that the new larger community may not value the same things, including liturgy and theology.

---

4 A multipoint parish or congregation has one or more congregations or buildings but is considered one financial or administrative unit served by one rector or incumbent.

While only a few clergy reported that their own local church population is in decline, some said that it is stable but aging, and others feel that, overall, the population of the Anglican Church is in decline. This is cause for concern, even among growing church communities, as they feel that a decline in the population in other areas will have an impact on their own requirements for financial support to the Church.

Some church communities feel that they could survive as an independent congregation if they were relieved of the expense of supporting the national Church. In both Vancouver and Red Deer, the issue of survival is, according to clergy, centred on the survival of the individual church communities and not the survival of the Anglican Church of Canada. Most clergy from church communities in both Vancouver and Red Deer indicated that *if* it were necessary for their church to "go it alone" to survive, then it would very likely do so. On the other hand, survival of the Anglican Church of Canada is a cause for some concern among clergy in Toronto and Newfoundland.

Financial concerns, lack of money, budgets, and survival of the local community church were mentioned in all communities, but the deepest concern was expressed in Toronto and Newfoundland. In both communities, the finances of the Church take a back seat to more general concerns about the economic impact of government cutbacks on services in their region. Concerns about the economic circumstance in their own regions are translated by their church communities into heightened awareness and action related to social justice.

Some active and growing churches are struggling to understand what value the Anglican Church of Canada brings to their local churches. Many feel protective of their own community, and defensive toward the Church. Local vision and the direction of the national Church are not often in sync.

Some feel that the national Church is important because it provides a link to worldwide Anglicanism. This is more important in urban church communities than in their rural counterparts. The link to worldwide Anglicanism is important in some of the urban churches because it provides a tangible link to new Canadians' Anglican traditions, as practised in the places of their birth.

Some church communities feel that they could do a more effective job of stewardship if they were able to make independent decisions about the ownership and management of properties. They feel it takes too long to get agreement through the management levels of the Church's hierarchy. Among less affluent church communities, there is some concern that the Church isn't up to date with the costs of maintaining church buildings and equipment, and that budgets and subsidies don't reflect the true costs. They worry that delays to repairs will add to costs.

Some feel that the diocesan level of the Church is failing to provide the leaders of the national Church with information about important issues at their local level. From a financial viewpoint, this leaves some church communities feeling that they are on their own, particularly in activities related to issues of social justice.

It is felt that no level of the Church is providing a way for church congregations with similar needs and interests to freely communicate, to get and share ideas.

The two factors generally thought to be the primary causes of the current financial circumstance of the Anglican Church of Canada are the settlement of litigation related to residential schools and the shortage of younger members.

***Issues:** Indigenous peoples' issues*
Healing and reconciliation

While a few urban churches continue to discuss Indigenous peoples' issues, for most this is "yesterday's news." It is not that anyone feels that the topic is unworthy of discussion, it is more that few people feel that they know enough about the topic to sustain discussion. Generally, there is agreement among clergy that the settlement issue is "out of the hands" of the Church, and is now with the courts.

Settlement of litigation and its economic impact on a particular church community is a topic for discussion, particularly among more affluent churches with more extensive lands and buildings, and among the least affluent in small communities with declining and aging populations. The discussion is not about Indigenous peoples; it has nothing to do with healing and reconciliation. The "issue" of residential schools is almost totally defined by its economic impact. Only a few church communities have discussed the moral or ethical issues, few understand the legal issues, and only a very few take any "ownership" at all for the circumstance. Indeed, the residential schools litigation creates a further divide between the local parish church community and the Anglican Church.

There is a wide spectrum of discussion. At one end, some said: "It isn't our fault. The federal government is to blame and should pay. We are just a third party." At the other end, some said: "How can people who have been so badly damaged ever learn to forgive?" In either case, the local church community sees itself as separate from this issue.

This separation from the issue makes it even more difficult for many church communities to willingly participate in settlements that they fear may bankrupt them. In affluent churches in Vancouver and small rural church communities in Alberta, clergy reported that some church parishes are looking at legal protection from "attachment of property."

The settlement of litigation related to residential schools has been very slow to happen, said many of the clergy. This lack of settlement, and of full disclosure of the impact that it will have on local church communities, has created at best, frustration, and at worst, mistrust.

There is also concern among some clergy that healing and reconciliation cannot succeed until litigation is settled. They are concerned that the issue among their parishioners is one of economics. Rather than healing and reconciliation, the economic cloud puts the survival of local church communities at odds with the settlement of past wrongs. Most of their parishioners, clergy reported, don't accept responsibility for the residential schools situation, and many resent the economic implications.

Issue: *The shortage of younger members of church communities*

The solution to declining membership most often mentioned is "to get more youthful people involved in church communities." Just how this might be done is the basis for divisive discussion. Some feel that the Anglican Church is "old-fashioned" and out of touch. Some feel that the evangelical arm of the Church has gone too far toward entertainment and away from worship. Some argue that participation in the Anglican Church has always been cyclical; people come and go at different times in their lives.

Clergy agree that leadership and direction related to youth and the Anglican Church are needed. The issue is particularly divisive between those who are involved in church communities that are more traditional and those that are more contemporary, and between the evangelical and the more liberal churches, as each type of church community has a very different vision of how youth might or should be encouraged to participate.

Anglican evangelical church populations are growing across all age sectors. Church communities that are more evangelical are more inclined than other churches to feel that they have something of value to offer to young people.

Traditional, contemporary, and liberal churches are more likely to feel that more young members in their church community would be "good business." These congregations are actively looking to find ways to attract and interest young people to come to their churches. Most clergy admit that the thought behind this effort is to increase the revenues in their local church accounts. Most church communities have not had much, if any, discussion about a relevant "ministry" related to youth.

Some members of the mainstream clergy said they and members of their congregation are trying to better understand the needs of those who are "missing from their population." They are less likely than the evangelical churches to feel that there is an easy fit for many of today's youth with the Anglican Church, and more likely to feel that secular activities are the biggest "competition" for youth participation in church communities. Some clergy feel that this is a real threat to the survival of church communities. Some feel at a loss as to how to reverse this trend in their own area. Secular competition was discussed in general in all communities, but was a specific and separate topic of concern in both Red Deer and St. John's rural areas.

Some feel that the search for "youth" members is a waste of time, as historically participation in the Anglican Church has been defined by lifestage. Those clergy who feel this to be true believe that when families are grown, adults who have an Anglican tradition will return to the Church and fill the roles of those who are currently "at the helm."

Evangelical churches of other denominations are considered by some clergy to be formidable competition. Parents of teens attend service at evangelical churches as well as the Anglican Church because their teens are involved in youth choirs and other activities at these churches, but take no part in the Anglican Church. Some worry that parents will leave the Anglican congregation to join the church community where their children go to worship.

Some feel that the worship service offered at evangelical churches is more akin to entertainment than worship. Some are disdainful of this approach, while others feel that there is joy in the music of many evangelical churches, and that this joy should be seen as a celebration of Christian belief and not dismissed as inappropriate worship. Some said that they feel that the Church should take a careful look at the relevance of evangelical churches to the people they serve.

Issue: *Diversity in worship*

Clergy from all regions across the county indicated that, within their own church communities, when the issue of "youth in the Church" is brought forward, the root of the discussion is not about youth at all, but rather about "old, but unresolved discussions" about traditional versus contemporary worship, evangelical versus liberal theology.

While many larger church communities have resolved issues around the use of the *Book of Common Prayer* versus the *Book of Alternative Services* by providing opportunities for parishioners to worship at different services held throughout their Sunday schedule, clergy told us that some smaller church communities are still struggling with this question.

However, the issues go beyond "the books." There are fundamental questions about what is truly Anglican: traditional versus contemporary, evangelism versus liberalism.

Many clergy feel that the Church should be providing more and better support to clergy as they seek to help their parishes deal with diversity, issues of inclusion, and tolerance.

Without vision and leadership, clergy and their congregations are concerned about the increasing fragmentation of the Church, and, through this fragmentation, the demise of the national Church in favour of congregationalism.

Most, but not all, clergy feel that there is room in the Anglican Church of Canada for diversity of liturgy and theology. However, many feel that it is important for the national Church to address these issues, rather than have them "fester" at the local community church level with no resolution.

If it is resolved that Anglicanism takes diverse forms, then this should be said. *If*, on the other hand, there are church communities that fall outside the acceptable form for the Anglican Church, they should be told. Clergy feel that if there were churches that fall into this category, these church communities would likely not find it surprising that they don't "fit," and they would "move on" and become independent congregations.

Issue: *Connection and responsibility*

Some clergy feel that the Church is very slow to become aware of issues that it should be addressing.

The key concern of many church communities is the role of their church related to social justice. Cutbacks in social services and changes in economic climate have created increased pressure on local church communities. Some church communities are struggling under the weight of their responsibility. Budgets are low, food and supplies are getting harder and harder to acquire, and volunteers are often nearing "burn-out."

Many feel that, beyond the physical help that they seek to achieve at a local level, the national Church could or should play a larger role as an advocate for social justice.

Some clergy reported pride among members of their church communities in British Columbia, where recently the bishops took a stand on the referendum. In Newfoundland, the bishop encouraged people to talk about their faith in a more public way, in an event called "Raise the Cross High." While some parishioners and clergy don't agree with the particular stands made by the bishops, there is, in most communities, a sense of pride that the Church is aware and taking action on issues important to their geographic area.

Issue: *Homosexuality*

In many church communities across Canada, homosexuality is not at the present time a subject of discussion. Clergy in all regions reported that about a year before this study, there was directed discussion in church communities about the inclusion of gays and lesbians into the life of the Church. Included in those discussions were issues about the inclusion of gays and lesbians through ordination, receiving sacraments, and blessing same-sex unions.

In many areas across the country, clergy told us that it is a non-issue in their church community as "there are no gay people in our area."

Some said that the discussion is embarrassing to them and to others, so it is mostly just avoided. A few said that they feel that the subject should never have been brought forward in the first place, as they believe that homosexuality is a sin and has no place in discussions of the Church. Most clergy outside urban Vancouver and urban Toronto reported that directed discussions were the only conversations about the issue in their church communities. In these communities, there is no ownership of the issue and few see that it has any relevance.

This is not the case in most urban and some suburban churches. Many urban and suburban clergy feel that this is a highly emotional topic for many in their church community and one that is very divisive in some communities. To avoid heated discussions about the issue, some congregations "side-step" the discussion, or deliberately "move to other topics" so as not to end up in angry debate.

While many urban church communities talk about tolerance, tolerance is a long way from inclusion. Some clergy tell us that there are those in their community who feel it is their Christian duty to be "tolerant" of different lifestyle choices, including homosexuality, but that some of their parishioners take the position that it is "going too far" to let "them" into all church sacraments. In these communities, the ordination of gay and lesbian clergy, the inclusion of gay and lesbian people in all sacraments, and the blessing of same-sex relationships are not considered worthy of discussion. It is, in these communities, a "closed case."

Other urban church communities take pride in being known as "gay-friendly." Their position is that full inclusion of gays and lesbians into the daily life of the community in all of its aspects is right and appropriate.

In still other church communities, the issue is less clear. Some clergy feel abandoned by the Church on this issue; some feel that they have not been given a clear vision of the Church's position. The confusion comes between "action and words." In British Columbia, the Synod voted in favour of blessing same-sex relationships; the bishop, however, decided that the time wasn't yet right. Some wonder why there was a vote if a decision had already been taken; others wonder when and under what circumstance the time will be right.

Some clergy advocate that an individual priest should be able to make a decision to bless a relationship or not, based on his or her own conscience, while others feel strongly that the Church should have a well-thought-out stand, and then back it up with programs to help priests to share the decision with their parishes.

Some clergy are concerned that the issue of blessing same-sex relationships has been discussed at the expense of the large and, from their viewpoint, more important issue of including gays and lesbians in the whole and active life of their church communities.

Among non-urban church communities, the topic is not often top-of-mind, and indeed, in some communities, it is avoided whenever possible. In many of the smaller church communities, homosexuality and sexual abuse become a single "hyphenated" topic.

Some clergy feel that they need help to separate the two topics and to bring the discussion to the table. Some feel that they are ill-equipped to discuss the topic, as they are unsure of their own position on the issue.

There is general agreement among clergy that this topic is one that has high potential to contribute to fragmentation in the Church.

Issue: *Church's leaders distracted*

In speaking for themselves, some clergy feel that the Church's leaders have been distracted by the residential schools issue and by the issue of inclusion of homosexuals into the active life of the church community. While all would agree that these are important issues, some feel that there has been too much time and discussion around the issues and that "solutions" are very slow in coming.

Some clergy worry that these two particular issues have taken such a predominant place in the day-to-day activities of the Church's leaders that they have lost touch with the needs and interests of other key areas of concern. Some describe the distraction of the leadership of the Church as having a "disconnect" between stewardship and the business of the Church, and actions of ministry.

Clergy reported that, in their own church communities, parishioners feel that the Anglican Church of Canada lacks vision, purpose, and leadership. Many feel that there are few "answers" from the Church to their questions, and that when issues are identified, there is little response, or the response they receive is too long in coming to be useful or effective.

What has been lost during this time of distraction, clergy tell us, is clear communication among various levels of the Church. They fear that this lack of communication is causing a breakdown in trust among all levels of the Church, even among parishes in the same diocese. They are troubled by inadequate support to local parish churches from their bishops, and by a lack of vision about the future of the national Church.

While without good stewardship, most feel that the Church will not survive, it worries some that the cost of survival may be the loss of liturgical and theological vision.

5.0 CONCERNS OF STAKEHOLDERS IN THE ANGLICAN COMMUNITY

5.1 Anglican Council of Indigenous Peoples (ACIP)

We met with the Anglican Council of Indigenous Peoples (ACIP) on April 14, 2002 in Edmonton, Alberta.

Members of the Anglican Council of Indigenous Peoples represent the wide diversity of the First Nations. They bring to the Council different cultures, language groups, and geography. The working language of the Council is English.

Members of the Council live in both reserve and non-reserve communities, with only a few living in other towns and cities across Canada.

The common characteristic of Council members is that they are also members of the Anglican community. In listening to their stories, we found that being an Anglican is not, in some of their communities, an easy thing to be.

This session was scheduled as a two-hour workshop on Saturday, April 14. However, the methodology changed from a specific talking circle over a short time, to an intense listening and observation session, running from 9:00 a.m. until 5:00 p.m.

This change occurred for two specific reasons. The first was that the questions intended for the special "talking circle" had been the essence of questions addressed in the "topic of discussion" during the full day *in camera* sessions the day before. The *in camera* sessions were called to allow Council members to talk freely without staff intervention, and to share information and concerns with each other that were felt to be too sensitive for the broader forum. By the time the Saturday session began, much of the atmosphere of secrecy and inhibition had been cleared. Many in the group appeared visibly tired and some were emotionally drained.

Those participating in the Saturday session reviewed here were fully engaged in sharing information, and were clear and articulate in expressing both their concerns and their excitement and enthusiasm.

Attendance ranged between 22 and 25 people. Some attended all day, some came into and out of the session from time to time, and a few attended the afternoon session but not the morning meeting. Those attending included representatives to the Council of Indigenous Peoples, their spouses, Anglican Church staff, and official observers. The composition of this Council session was described to us as typical for the ACIP.

As the specific stories revealed in this session often included personally identifying information, this account contains few verbatim comments.

The text summary is intended to provide the reader with insights into the stories and concerns presented by members of the ACIP. In the telling of their stories and experience in the talking circle, members of the ACIP share the context in which they confront the issues under discussion in their day-to-day lives, as well as how this "fits" into their relationship with the Anglican Church of Canada.

Issue: *The key, overriding concern is the survival of individuals, their families, and their communities*

Finding sustainable economic opportunities for communities is of paramount importance. Many reported that their communities are working hard to be able to free themselves from a "victim" posture. The key ingredient for self-reliance, if not self-determination, will require that communities find meaningful and lucrative employment for members of their respective communities.

The loss of mining, logging, hunting, fishing, and other common income-earning activities in the North has made the situation ever more difficult. Many of the communities suffer from "closed economies," that is, what little money there is in the community is circulated around and around within the community, with little "new money" being introduced.

Some members of the Council also work for their band councils. Employment with the band council is good and steady employment, but pays only a minimum income. To supplement their incomes, many also engage in other entrepreneurial activities. They have "home parties" for all manner of things from housewares to clothing; they work as contractors, babysitters, construction workers, teachers, and administrators.

Fishing and hunting supplement expensive purchased food.

Alcoholism among adults and gas sniffing among teens and young adults are common.

Boredom and despair are often part of the "texture" of daily life, particularly in remote communities.

Like their counterparts in Newfoundland, many on the Council worry because many young people are leaving their communities to find employment and opportunity far away from home.

Many worry that if they are not able to find sustainable economic solutions, their communities will die.

Issue: *Longing for hope and vision*

Joy and enthusiasm, hope and vision are taken in "small bites" and then tempered by past disappointing experience. The tempering allows disappointment to be less harsh. Yet there is hope to be found in the Church:

- *A hope for inclusion*: the Anglican Church seeks representation from Indigenous voices
- *A hope for inclusion*: committee reports on joint worship continue with the Council of General Synod
- *A hope for vision*: the development of an action plan — how do Indigenous peoples fit into the Church's agenda?
- *A hope for vision and a hope for movement from special to equal status*: Council of the North — Healing and Reconciliation Fund
- *A hope for learning*: Elders to provide "light from a different direction"

Issues: *Moving from special status to equal status*
Healing and reconciliation

The issue of stipendiary and non-stipendiary priests was one of the key issues discussed in the *in camera* meeting of the day before the Council session that was observed in this study. This issue anchored the "talking circle" in this session of the ACIP. Much of the discussion in this session was part of preliminary preparation for a presentation to the House of Bishops.

One of the key issue areas was related to special funds for the North.[5] Some wonder if perhaps the bishops don't understand the harsh realities of ministry in the North.

- They wonder why money from the Fund doesn't seem to be available to local/individual Indigenous ministries.
- They wonder how the Fund is distributed and who makes these decisions.
- What makes one Indigenous ministry more appealing to the Fund than another?
- To whom is the Fund accountable? And what are the "rules" under which the Fund operates?

Several members of the Council told stories in support of their concerns about unfair or uninformed decisions that are taken by the bishops re-

5 The General Synod of the Anglican Church of Canada funds work in the North through a grant to the Council of the North. The Council of the North was established in 1976 and comprises all bishops of assisted dioceses. The grant is allocated by the Council to assisted dioceses to support the work of these dioceses and their parishes.

lated to stipends for those who are responsible for various ministries within individual communities of Indigenous peoples.

While most understand and appreciate that the Fund does pay for infrastructure of the Church, many believe that very few dollars are spent in support of ministry. Some ask, "How can you run a ministry with no money and no food to those who minister?"

The stories tell of the desperate economic circumstances in which many members of the Council live, and the "price" they pay for being active members of their Anglican community. Some spoke of "being taunted" by other members of their community for working on behalf of the Church. Some spoke of living on welfare, of having food provided by other members of their community so that they could do their work for the Church.

Some spoke about entering their work believing that they would "partner" with a priest in bringing the Church to the people of their community, and then finding that supplies, materials, and equipment that they require to do their job will not be available to them. The things that they need are under lock and key, housed in their own community, sitting idle between visits by the "real priest."

Examples are given of communities where there are two priests, one who is from the community and one who is not. They talk about how upset the community is when the local priest must be given food from the community because they can't afford to buy it, while the "other priest" lives comfortably. Many don't understand why they are not treated more equally.

Some told of having to go on welfare to survive, living on the generosity of the community for food (mostly wild game meat), even buying candles for services out of their own pocket so as not to bother the bishop.

Some told of driving long distances to have wine blessed, and paying more than half of the costs of transportation out of their own pockets, because the allowable amount is insufficient to cover the trip (it was down to 12 cents per kilometre, and is now back up to 24 cents).

Among those with a stipend, we heard of the stipend being used as a weapon: "I give you your stipend — remember you owe me."

Some spoke of being treated with little respect or consideration by priests and others in the Anglican Church. They told of trying to arrange meetings with priests to discuss family crises of members of their community and being denied time. Some feel that rather than the other clergy understanding, that these conversations were seen as "consultations." Some feel that their attempts to bring the non-Indigenous clergy closer to the lives of the people in the community were rebuffed, as gossip, "telling tales." Some feel stretched "almost beyond endurance."

Among those who feel this way, many reported that they have had a lifelong commitment to the Anglican Church.

Many said that, rather than feeling that this is a time of "healing and reconciliation," they feel that it is a time of abandonment and denial.

While the imminent settlement of the residential schools litigation is seen by some as an opportunity for "new beginnings," others feel that it won't make a significant difference to the lives of Indigenous peoples. Some feel that settlement will be viewed by the House of Bishops as an "end of the problem" rather than as a beginning of a new relationship.

This is an important distinction for many, as the settlement will not, many believe, make a significant difference to the lives of Indigenous peoples or to the communities in which they live. Most agree that significant positive change must come from the people themselves, not from outside intervention. Some look to the Anglican Church to play a meaningful role in this positive change.

For this to work, we were told, the Church needs to "teach" non-Indigenous peoples to behave differently — not just to speak differently. Specifically, we were told that, while the Church speaks of "partnering" with Indigenous peoples in this time of healing and recognition, the behaviour of those who represent the Church to Indigenous peoples continues to be patronizing. Perhaps, some suggested, it is time to move away from "special status to equal status."

Included in this concept of equality are the following ideas:

- If the House of Bishops doesn't have a formula for determining priests' salaries, then one should be established.
- If the House of Bishops has a "scale" that it uses to define salary for stipendiary and non-stipendiary priests, then this scale should be "public knowledge" and take into consideration the skills, experience, and education of those being rated as well as relevant geographic considerations.

The Council does not appear to be asking for a "special scale" for those who minister in the North among Indigenous peoples, but rather a "scale" that is established for their own and other ministries where similar circumstance may exist.

The issue here is that most feel that the current decisions are being made in a vacuum and at the whim of administrators rather than with some more objective measures in place. They see no reason that this information should be "secret," if indeed there are objective measures.

Issue: *Cultural diversity among Indigenous communities*

Two key issues were discussed related to cultural diversity among Indigenous communities:

- "Symbols" of specific Indigenous communities are often selected to represent all Indigenous cultures. There seems to be a lack of sensitivity to the diversity of cultures and cultural icons within the Indigenous communities in Canada.
- Care should be taken within the Anglican Church to provide opportunities for Indigenous peoples to share their individual cultural iconography as they feel it is appropriate. When the Anglican Church seeks to incorporate the symbols of Indigenous peoples, there should be more consultation with members of diverse communities to ensure that the symbols are used in an appropriate and meaningful context.

Part of the discussion:

> "A while ago, a 'smudge pot' was used at the Cathedral in a service. It was an important event for the Anglican Church and particularly important for Indigenous peoples. I was surprised, and maybe just a bit insulted, by that smudge pot. This is not part of my culture at all."

> "I think that we all have to be very careful that we don't fall into creating new stereotypes that are no better than 'cowboy and Indian' movies. Our cultures do have an important place in our worship, as do the cultures of all other Anglicans. But these symbols need to be very carefully considered, not just selected for their dramatic effect, but rather for their spiritual significance and meaning across Indigenous cultures and traditions. I don't think this has been given enough thought. I also wonder if Indigenous peoples have been a meaningful part of these discussions at all."

Issue: *Membership in the Council of Indigenous Peoples*

To ensure that the diversity of culture and experience is represented in the ACIP, some feel that there should be better geographic representation.

Some have particular concerns about ministry for Indigenous peoples living in urban areas across the country.

> "I've heard that there are maybe 50,000 Indigenous peoples living in Toronto. That is a lot of people. We talk about ministry in our own communities, but what about for our people who are living in cities?"

Issue: *Incorporation of the Anglican Council of Indigenous Peoples*

Discussions about the role of the ACIP within the Anglican Church included discussions about the management of administration and finance issues, in part through incorporation. The topic of incorporation was originally considered to be part of the intended presentation to the House of Bishops. This was briefly debated and then the topic of incorporation was set aside for future consideration.

Issue: *Evangelistic versus traditional/conservative versus liberal*

Within the Council, discussions related to both liturgy and theology suggested that the positions on these issues mirror those of the non-Indigenous Anglican church communities. As with their counterparts outside the ACIP, they seek direction and vision from the Anglican Church of Canada on these issues.

Generally, members of the ACIP indicated that they believe that, as there is room in the Anglican Church for the diversity of Indigenous cultures and languages, there is also room for diversity in liturgy and theology. What is missing is a way of sharing and embracing this diversity as a "gift" rather than as a problem.

Issues: *Moving toward real healing*
Angry community members —" love of victimization"

The issues of self-determination, consistent non-patronizing interaction with non-Indigenous communities and strategies for reaching equal rather than special status are thought by many to be crucial to the survival of intact healthy Indigenous communities.

Some feel that the anger of some community members, both within and outside the Church, may be a symptom of a deeper issue. It was said that many people in Indigenous communities have become so accustomed to being "victims" that it has become part of their identity. It is felt that this identity of victimization needs to be stopped if a status of equals among equals is ever to be achieved for Indigenous peoples in Canada and in the Anglican Church.

5.2 Anglican Council of General Synod (COGS)

A facilitated workshop was conducted with members of the Anglican Council of General Synod in May 2002. Approximately 42 members of the Anglican Council of General Synod and staff attended a two-hour workshop session. The workshop was conducted within the structured schedule for the Council. Members of Council had been told that the workshop would be conducted and were prepared for the change in meeting "style" from that which they had been using for other sessions.

Those participating did so with energy and enthusiasm. The sharing of ideas seemed to be comfortable for most on Council. This suggests that the Council is accustomed to hearing ideas and views thar may be different or new. Generally, there seemed to be an openness to the full exchange of ideas.

The Council of General Synod is, in part, responsible for policy and accountability related to the finances of the Church. For this reason, it is not surprising that many of the key issues mentioned by the Council were indeed related to money, budgets, and stewardship of land and properties.

Many members of COGS indicated that Church properties are an important point of pride among the church communities they represent. Many told us that, in their own church communities, ensuring financial stability for maintenance of church buildings, cemeteries, parking lots, and other land holdings is considered very important.

5.2.1 Joy, Enthusiasm, Hope, Vision

Many church communities are defined, at least in part, by the church structure that is the symbol of their church community. Many take obvious pride in the physical aspects of the particular church that they attend, or, for example, in a cathedral that is at the centre of diocesan life.

Some feel that that they hear more people in their own church communities talking about their quest for more or different spiritual direction. Some said that it seems that there is a new willingness to share concerns and interests about issues of ethics, philosophy, theology, and spirituality. There is more discussion and sharing, and less preaching.

Many mentioned that, in various ways, the music in their church communities has improved and, as the music improves, people in their church communities are commenting that services are more interesting and engaging.

Some feel that, among those who attend church, many are interested in doing more than taking up space in a pew. This new interest in taking on a more active role in the life of the Church is seen by some to be a "gift." Activities of church members include the volunteer "work of the Church," as well as a renewed interest in some communities for Bible study and peer support groups.

While some churches worry about their church communities' survival because there are too few young people attending, other churches feel hope and joy because they find themselves with a growing Sunday school.

Some feel that the Anglican Church is, at this moment in time, more willing than ever to explore new models of ministry, consider new reforms, even to think about new ways of being a church.

Some feel that the evangelical movement within the Church has moved the whole Church toward a willingness to talk about God and the Gospel more directly.

Some feel that prayer is no longer only part of the Anglican Sunday liturgy, but is also becoming a more meaningful part of the daily lives of people.

Some feel that the Church is beginning to take much needed action in terms of social justice.

5.2.2 Concerns Within the Church/Concerns Outside the Church

The concerns held by Council participants, on issues both within and outside the Anglican Church (or their own church community) were thought, by Council members, to be mostly the same as the concerns and issues of those who are outside the Church.

Within the Council of General Synod, issues related to the relevance of the Anglican Church of Canada, including styles and forms of liturgy, and the spectrum of theology (evangelical or traditional, conservative or liberal), are often discussed.

One of the biggest concerns for the future is related to issues of social justice. Cutbacks in government spending, and how church communities might best help, are key issues for some church communities. Members of Anglican church communities are working in soup kitchens, in urban missions, at food banks, at shelters, and in school breakfast programs. Many volunteers are stressed and worn down by their work and the ever-increasing demands on their time and energy.

Cutbacks in the number of Anglican church communities worry some, as do changes in the service of priests in some areas. These concerns centre more on not liking change, than on the changes having had any adverse effect.

Some, but not all, church communities are worried about money and the survival of the Anglican Church. They worry primarily about the impact of economic pressure on the Anglican Church of Canada. Some are concerned that the Church will be bankrupted by residential school settlements. Will their church community survive through the readjustments that seem inevitable?

In small towns and rural areas, as well as in Newfoundland and among Indigenous communities, young people are leaving their home communities to find work in other places. Church communities worry that often there is a "hole" in their communities' populations — from teens through young adults. Many worry that if their church community is unable to attract "youth," then the community will surely die off.

Others say that it is the normal cycle of the Anglican Church; young people explore secular activities in their teens and as young single adults. Many feel that when people are in their 30s and 40s, they begin to drift back to the Church.

Some others feel that the key reason for fewer young people in the Anglican Church is that the Church is not relevant to them. They think that many young people would find the service dull and boring, and the music unappealing.

Some feel that *if* a church community wants to attract more young people, then there must be programs and events to capture their interest. Others argue that this has the potential of moving the activities of the Church from "religion and worship" into entertainment.

When asked directly, some indicated that their own church community has talked about separating from the Anglican Church of Canada. Some of these church communities reported that they feel that they have no financial reasons to stay in the Church, and that the Church no longer provides links to other organizations of the Church.

Some said that those in their church community are unclear about the nature of the "benefits" of being an Anglican, as many have only rarely worshipped outside their own community.

Some are concerned that the Church has lost the proper balance between stewardship and ministry. While most feel that this imbalance has occurred because of the residential schools litigation, they wonder if and how this imbalance will be addressed. Will the settlement of the litigation actually be a time when the Church can reassess its role in ministry as well as stewardship? A few feel that the Anglican Church of Canada is now all about the business of the Church, while the church communities that are part of the Church have been abandoned to figure out questions of ministry on their own, with little leadership and little vision from the Church.

In most church communities, the issues of residential schools, misconduct, sexual abuse, drugs, sex, homosexuality, family breakdown, etc. are not currently being discussed. These topics are clearly uncomfortable ones for many people, and so, in many church communities the subjects are only "brought forward" when there is an instruction to do so. In some church communities, it has been 18 months or longer since these issues were "on the table."

Several members of COGS said "we had homosexuality in our discussions about 18 months ago — maybe a year ago. I think that was the last time. It isn't very interesting to us, as we don't have any gays or lesbians in our community."

For many, it is not that these topics are considered inappropriate or that they are not worthy of discussion. It is that they are uncomfortable topics to address. Some told us that many priests don't have the skills or "tools" to address these issues with their congregations. Some said that priests are uncomfortable "teaching" without guidance and vision.

We were told that, as with many "sensitive topics," unless there is some sort of instructional material from the Anglican Church of Canada or from a bishop's office, when a topic is beyond their experience, many will avoid the subject. Some indicated that clergy and laity don't have a resource for adult education on sensitive issues. A few thought that this might be a role for their bishop. Many feel that leadership training is needed for both clergy and laity to help them to be more professional in their approaches to sensitive subjects. Now, without the benefit of such training, sensitive subjects are "side-stepped" or ignored by church communities because there is no one to facilitate the discussions.

Homosexuality, inclusion of gays and lesbians into the daily life of the Church, the ordination of gays and lesbians, gays and lesbians and the sacraments within the Church, and the blessing of same-sex relationships are current topics of open discussion primarily in some large urban churches.

In many other church communities, the topic of homosexuality is not about inclusion, but rather gets linked either to discussions about the residential schools litigation or to discussions about sexual abuse. In many church communities, the topic is simply avoided whenever possible. In some, this means that the subject is just not discussed at all.

Some feel that a positive decision related to the blessing of same-sex unions would be a dramatic step toward a vision of inclusion and tolerance. Some feel that this is among the most divisive topics in the Church today. Few feel that they have been given leadership or vision related to this issue, and many wonder why this is so.

5.3 Huron Youth Synod

We met with members of the Huron Youth Synod in London, Ontario, on May 24, 2002. The Huron Youth Synod is made up of teens from church communities in the Huron Diocese. Participants in this weekend event came from London, as well as smaller rural communities in the area.

This event was centred on a classroom style lecture format. In addition to the classes, participants had time to meet other Anglican teens and to socialize. The group graciously allowed a two-hour break in their program and agenda for this "intentional listening" session. The session ran from about 4:00 p.m. until 6:00 p.m. Approximately 42 teens attended this session, with a few coming and going throughout the session. The youth leaders participated, but worked in a team separate from the teens themselves.

At the time we met with the group, on a Saturday afternoon, most had been together for over 24 hours. The boys had spent the night on the floor of the host church Sunday school area, while the girls had stayed in the rectory. Just before the intentional listening session, the teens had been for a swim and shower.

Generally, all of those present participated with energy, and most were willing and eager to share their ideas. As the session neared 6:00 p.m., the wonderful smell of baked lasagne was a clear distraction. The teens were all hungry and ready to move on to the evening's social events.

5.3.1 The Practical "Listening" of Youth

Many teens indicated that they were "listeners" rather than active participants in the conversations within their own church communities. Most feel that the ideas and thoughts of young people are not very important to the adults in their congregations.

They talked about their own activities and experiences, and those of youth in general, within their church communities:

- Most indicated that the involvement of youth in their church community includes teaching Sunday school, singing in the choir, and helping with programs for "younger kids." Only a very few churches have active youth programs, events, or classes.
- Many of the Huron Youth indicated that their church communities (adults) were talking about how they might get more young people into the church community.

- Some communities have discussed hiring youth outreach workers or raising funds to support programs for young people. The "problem" with moving forward with these discussions is that there just aren't that many young people who would want to come to an Anglican Church program, according to teens in the Council. The reason for this, from the teens' perspective, is that if they are involved in a church already, it is probably because of their family's choice of church or because they have already chosen to attend activities at other churches.
- Some reported that they are actively involved in Christian youth programs run by other evangelical churches in their area. Some reported that it is great fun to socialize with other Christian teens who share the same interests and values. They went on to say that while they enjoy this social time, it is not "worship."
- Most worship at an Anglican church along with other members of their families.

Teens reported the following matters are now, or have recently been, the topic of conversation among the adults in their church communities:

- Wheelchair accessibility has been the cause of fundraising in a few communities. As the population of the church community is aging, some have decided that it is time to make their church buildings accessible.
- In addition to accessibility, the "well-being" of older church members is a topic of conversation in some churches. This includes volunteers who visit, and some who prepare or deliver meals to those who can no longer do it for themselves.
- In some church communities, there have been recent and ongoing redecorating and renovation projects. This is a common activity in the spring in some of the smaller church communities.
- One church community has been installing a new security system after a robbery. There have been discussions about changing morality and how sad it is that a church would be robbed. The need for the security system was established, fundraising was conducted, and now the system is being installed.
- Some church communities have Bible study or discussions about faith and God. While most of the teens do not attend these discussions themselves, they hear about the classes and generally reported that those participating seem to find the classes and discussions interesting.

- "Old people" gossip a lot in many of the church communities, the teens told us.
- Some reported that adults in their church community also discuss the changing morality of youth. At this point in the conversation, a few also mentioned that, as teens, they often discuss the "generation gap" between the adults of their church and youth. The generation gap includes issues as varied as technology, fashion, education, stress, and the use of alcohol.

Other topics discussed in the teens' church communities include:

- Local financial concerns about church buildings and land maintenance, and other money to support church activities, programs, and obligations to the diocese and to the Anglican Church of Canada.
- Fundraising is getting more difficult in some church communities as so many different community-based "services" are no longer adequately funded. The local library, sports programs for young people, music programs in schools, and other services have been stopped. All of these require fundraising in addition to the church communities' activities.
- Government cutbacks to social services, health care, and schools.
- A few said that their churches are running or are involved with local food banks and shelters for homeless people. Only a very few had been involved in these outreach activities themselves.
- Some said that they have listened to discussions about the mission of the Church, although few were clear what exactly the mission is, or what those in their church community thought it should be.

In thinking about the things that are of concern to their age cohorts and others outside the Church, the following topic areas were mentioned:

- Most teen conversations are about their own day-to-day lives and those of other teens. They talk with their friends about school sports, fashion, popular music, technology, gaming on-line, movies, dances, school events and activities, learning to drive, etc. They also talk about other teens.
- They talk about drugs and alcohol; love, sex, and sexually transmitted diseases; work/jobs, career, and their future; school, university, and leaving home.
- Some said that they are interested in talking to their friends about "alternative spirituality," which includes Wicca.

- There is concern over the economy, and the stability of their own families' finances.
- Since September 11th, there are many conversations and discussions about war and terrorism.
- Some reported that, since September 11th, they have heard more racist comments, and that there seems to be a spirit that is less tolerant of others' religions and cultures than before. Racism and prejudice are part of more conversations than in the past.
- There have been discussions about books and television programs that explain Islam. Few had thought about what it means to be a Muslim before September 11th.
- There are also discussions about genetically-modified animals and produce. These conversations are centred on issues of safety first, followed by "ethics."
- Education is, among teens, a very personal topic. They discuss how the "double cohort" in Ontario will impact on their future university studies and on the job market in general. Most think it is a poor idea. Most feel that they are experiencing personal stress because of the change in policy.

What teens want, more than anything else, is to be respected within their church communities. They want to be participants more often than observers.

They would like to see more church-related or church-sponsored events and activities geared to teens, but not necessarily in their local community church.

They would like to have more opportunities to meet other Anglican teens, to share ideas and fellowship.

AFTERWORD

The stories told by participants in this study were full of rich and meaningful images. Asked to share their concerns and their visions, their stories of enthusiasm, excitement, despair and hope, they spoke with honesty and courage, commitment, and faith.

For many in the Canadian Anglican tradition, "traditional" forms of worship, in a traditional and familiar environment, bring peace, comfort, and joy. Some spoke about the light through the stained glass windows of their home church, how the colour and light weave into the very fabric of their spiritual experience. Many found a comfortable connection to their faith community in the traditional materials of Anglican worship. For some, their sense perception of the physical church environment is a significant part of their worship and prayer experience. The smell of starch as they iron a vestment or an altar cloth, a whiff of spent wax when they put out a candle, the sound of a slightly off-key piano, the tap of feet walking down a stone or wooden aisle before the service begins, are for some a very real and tangible part of how they experience their faith. Even the texture of the wood in their home church pew, the familiar feel of the pages in their book of prayer, are part of how some feel grounded in their faith. Some are troubled by the thought that these symbols of faith made manifest might change, or even be lost. Others look around them, see pews half-empty, and worry about the future of the Church itself.

For many Anglicans from outside the Canadian tradition, these common objects of the Canadian Anglican Church are not familiar. They come to the Church from other Anglican traditions, ones where the churches look and feel and sound different from mainstream churches in Canada. Some long for other traditions, those of their home Anglican culture, the music, the familiar perfumes, the textures. Some come from mission church cultures; others are firmly rooted in the idea of church communities that adapt forms of worship to ensure relevance to current life.

Some Anglicans who worship with church communities that are somehow "outside the mainstream" say that the rhythm of their own worship tradition just does not move at the same pace as does the Anglican tradition in Canada. Some say that the rhythm of worship in the mainstream Church can be troubling and, for some, even foreign to their sense of faith and worship.

Some Anglicans, gays and lesbians, worship in church communities even as they engage in dialogue with the Church over their place within it. Some even worship in church communities where they are not welcome, witnesses by their very presence to their belief that there is a place for them in their Church, and that only through commitment to community will it be found.

For many Indigenous Anglicans, the key concerns continue to be survival issues for their communities — development of sustainable economic opportunities, better access to medical care, better access to education for both children and adults — rather than issues of the Anglican Church. Indigenous Anglican communities face the reality of a shrinking and aging population, the result, they say, of secular demands on time and energy as well as successful fundamentalist evangelical mission churches membership drives. This makes those who are working hard to keep the Anglican Church alive in their communities very sad.

Some feel that they are not being given appropriate support by the Anglican Church of Canada. Others feel that in its attempt to be responsive to the needs of Indigenous peoples, the Church has been less than sensitive to the imagery and symbols of faith and worship as they vary across different Indigenous cultures. There is concern within the Indigenous Council that the multicultural aspect of Indigenous cultures is either not well understood or being ignored.

No matter how diverse the concerns and fears expressed, mingled among them were voices that spoke in harmony with each other about the importance of faith and celebration and the spiritual journey. And all across Canada, people reported signs of joy: new music and new musical skills have become part of some churches for the first time, or after having been absent for a long time; among evangelical churches there are growing populations, including young families; among some mainstream churches there is a sense of commitment to participate in programs for social justice; among some Church members there is a commitment to seeking a path toward spiritual learning.

Debate and discussion, we are told, are often considered by Anglicans to be part of the "family characteristics." Those who came to participate in this study did so with great openness and a clear interest in learning from each other, as well as putting forward their own ideas and agenda. It is telling that at the end of each session, while not often in complete agreement with others participating in these discussions, those attending would come together in prayer.

At the end of sessions, participants often commented on how they feel about being an Anglican and what they hope for the future. Their words underline both their sense of a unity in faith and spirit that encompasses and transcends the diversity of their experience, and their trust in their Church and in each other:

> "It is good to know that wherever you might be, you could likely find another Anglican. Even if every Anglican Church does things a bit different from another one, we are Anglicans; we have a common spiritual home. I hope we can keep that." *Man, urban Vancouver*

> "Sometimes, even if we don't agree, it is good to know that there is a community of faith. I'm just sure that together we can find a way through all this." *Woman, rural Newfoundland*

APPENDIX A

THE ANGLICAN CHURCH OF CANADA

Primate of the Anglican Church of Canada

The Most Rev. Michael G. Peers

Bishop Ordinary to the Canadian Forces

The Most Rev. Andrew S. Hutchison

ECCLESIASTICAL PROVINCES AND DIOCESES

PROVINCE OF CANADA

Metropolitan, The Most Rev. Andrew S. Hutchison

Dioceses

Central Newfoundland
Eastern Newfoundland and Labrador
Fredericton
Montreal
Nova Scotia and Prince Edward Island
Quebec
Western Newfoundland

PROVINCE OF ONTARIO

Metropolitan, The Most Rev. Terence E. Finlay

Dioceses

Algoma
Huron
Moosonee
Niagara
Ontario
Ottawa
Toronto

PROVINCE OF RUPERT'S LAND

Metropolitan, The Most Rev. Thomas O. Morgan

Dioceses

Arctic
Athabasca
Brandon
Calgary
Edmonton
Keewatin
Qu'Appelle
Rupert's Land
Saskatchewan
Saskatoon

PROVINCE OF BRITISH COLUMBIA AND YUKON

Metropolitan, The Most Rev. David P. Crawley

Dioceses

The Anglican Parishes of the Interior
British Columbia
Caledonia
Kootenay
New Westminster
Yukon

THE ANGLICAN CHURCH OF CANADA

Who Are We?

The Anglican Church is a community of worshipping Christians, with more than 70 million members around the world. In Canada, our church is called the Anglican Church of Canada. In other countries, it may be known as the Church of England or Episcopal Church. The Most Rev. Rowan Williams was appointed to succeed Dr. George Carey as the 104th Archbishop of Canterbury and the head of the worldwide Anglican Communion in July 2002.

The Anglican Church is divided into regional groupings called "dioceses." Each diocese has its own bishop (or bishops), who have the overall responsibility for the spiritual well-being and administration of the churches within the area.

In Canada, more than 700,000 Anglicans worship in 29 dioceses, from Vancouver Island to St. John's, Newfoundland, and from the country's southernmost part to the Arctic Circle. The Most Rev. Michael Peers is the head (called the "Primate") of the national church. The Anglican Church of Canada supports churches in large urban areas, small rural villages, and in remote northern regions. In addition to English, worship is conducted in many other languages, including French, Spanish, Cantonese, Japanese, Mandarin, as well as Indigenous languages.

Governance

Every three years, approximately 300 representatives from dioceses across the country gather together at a meeting called General Synod ("synod" meaning "the common road" or "the road together") to make decisions about the national work of the church. Between Synods, a group called the Council of General Synod is authorized to make decisions on behalf of the wider church. Other counsel or advice is given by the "House of Bishops" — a gathering of bishops and archbishops from across Canada who meet regularly to consult with each other on spiritual, moral, and leadership issues.

How Is the Church Organized?

The Anglican Church consists of lay persons, deacons, priests, and bishops. We consider all baptized Christians to be "ministers," as they share their gifts and talents. However, some members of the Church feel called to be ordained as deacons, priests, or bishops. In the Anglican Church of Canada, both women and men are eligible for ordination.

Deacons serve as a bridge between church and community. Often employed outside the church, deacons help to interpret the needs and concerns of society to church leaders, and help to support and nurture church members. There are two kinds of deacons — transitional deacons, who serve in this role for an interim period before being ordained to the priesthood, and vocational deacons, who choose the diaconate as a lifelong ministry.

The priest serves as a pastor and teacher to members of the church, is responsible for worship, preaches, and supports members of the congregation as they reach out into their community. Some priests find their vocation in a non-church setting, such as a hospital, university, or prison chaplaincy.

Bishops are elected by priests and lay people. They provide leadership and care for groups of congregations (a diocese) and serve as a link with the mission and ministry of the national and international church and with other faith traditions.

When bishops are elected to exercise oversight for a larger constituency within the Church, such as an Ecclesiastical Province or as head of a national church, they receive the title Archbishop.

Our History

The Anglican tradition goes back to the 6th century, when Christianity was re-established in the British Isles. It began to emerge as a distinct denomination in the 16th century, during a turbulent period of reform in the Church. Anglican reformers chose a "middle way" between the Roman Catholicism of the time and the various forms of Protestantism that developed in Europe during the Reformation. There were two main stages in the spread of Anglicanism — the first in the 17th century, during the colonization of the United States, Canada, Australia, New Zealand, and South Africa. The second stage began in the 18th century, when missionaries travelled to Asia, Africa, and South America to spread the Gospel and to establish churches.

Today the Anglican Church continues to strive to offer a middle way. While the Church presents clear, biblically based teaching and guidance on most subjects, we also understand that there are some issues in life that can be experienced and interpreted in different ways by different people. We encourage respectful listening, dialogue rather than debate, and "unity in diversity" among our members as we seek to live faithful and fruitful lives.

THE SOLEMN DECLARATION OF 1893

In the name of the Father, and of the Son, and of the Holy Ghost. Amen.

WE, the Bishops, together with the Delegates from the Clergy and Laity of the Church of England in the Dominion of Canada, now assembled in the first General Synod, hereby make the following Solemn Declaration:

WE declare this Church to be, and desire that it shall continue, in full communion with the Church of England throughout the world, as an integral portion of the One Body of Christ composed of the Churches which, united under the One Divine Head and in fellowship of the One Holy Catholic and Apostolic Church, hold the One Faith revealed in Holy Writ, and defined in the Creeds as maintained by the undivided primitive Church in the undisputed Ecumenical Councils; receive the same Canonical Scriptures of the Old and New Testaments, as containing all things necessary to salvation; teach the same Word of God; partake of the same Divinely ordained Sacraments, through the ministry of the same Apostolic Orders; and worship One God and Father through the same Lord Jesus Christ, by the same Holy and Divine Spirit who is given to them that believe to guide them into all truth.

And we are determined by the help of God to hold and maintain the Doctrine, Sacraments, and Discipline of Christ as the Lord hath commanded in his Holy Word, and as the Church of England hath received and set forth the same in *The Book of Common Prayer and Administration of the Sacraments and other Rites and Ceremonies of the Church, according to the use of the Church of England; together with the Psalter or Psalms of David, pointed as they are to be sung or said in Churches; and the Form and Manner of Making, Ordaining, and Consecrating of Bishops, Priests, and Deacons;* and in the Thirty-Nine Articles of Religion; and to transmit the same unimpaired to our posterity.

from The Book of Common Prayer (1959), *Canada*

APPENDIX B
Mission Statement of the Anglican Church of Canada

The Anglican Church of Canada
MISSION STATEMENT

As a partner in the worldwide Anglican Communion and in the universal Church, we proclaim and celebrate the Gospel of Jesus Christ in worship and action.

We value our heritage of biblical faith, reason, liturgy, tradition, bishops and synods, and the rich variety of our life in community.

We acknowledge that God is calling us to greater diversity of membership, wider participation in ministry and leadership, better stewardship in God's creation, and a strong resolve in challenging attitudes and structures that cause injustice.

Guided by the Holy Spirit, we commit ourselves to respond to this call in love and service and so more fully live the life of Christ.

L' Église anglicane du Canada
ÉNONCÉ DE MISSION

En tant que partenaires à part entière de la communion anglicane internationale et de l'Église universelle, nous proclamons et célébrons l'Évangile de Jésus-Christ par notre liturgie et nos gestes.

Nous accordons une place de choix à notre héritage composé de notre foi biblique, de raison, de liturgie, de tradition, de notre épiscopat et de nos synodes, et de la grande richesse de notre vie en communauté.

Nous reconnaissons que Dieu nous appelle à une plus grande diversification dans notre communauté chrétienne, à une participation plus étendue dans le ministère et dans les prises de décision, à un engagement plus profond dans la création que Dieu nous a confiée, et à une remise en question des attitudes et des structures qui causent des injustices.

Guidés par l'Esprit Saint, nous nous engageons à répondre à ces appels avec amour et esprit de service, vivant ainsi plus profondément la vie du Christ.

APPENDIX C
Preparing the Way — A Strategic Plan

adopted June 1995 by the 34th General Synod
with revision adopted by General Synod 2001

Priorities and Corresponding Approaches

A. Strengthen our mission and development partnerships outside Canada

National

In accordance with the Anglican Communion's *10 Principles of Partnership*, seek to learn from our partners and focus our resources to enable local autonomy.

1. Create stronger, mutually beneficial worldwide partnerships
2. Target specific regions overseas for priority partnership work (e.g., Tanzania)
3. Link companion dioceses to targeted regions
4. Expand Volunteers in Mission program to include an increased educational component
5. Provide funds to the extent possible
6. Facilitate networks for education, advocacy
7. Increase collaboration between committees engaged in international work (e.g., fund-raising, education, networking, and advocacy)

Diocesan and Parish

Increase visibility and participation; support financially
1. Encourage coordinated creative work in education and fund-raising for world mission and development
2. Encourage dissemination of information about world partners
3. Identify and uphold network volunteers — seek potential volunteers in mission; seek placement for external volunteers in Canada
4. Connect ecumenically re: international work
5. Engage actively in companion dioceses relationship

B. Clarify Anglican identity, doctrine, liturgy, and worship

National

Co-ordinate standards for worship, liturgy, and ministry; initiate theological dialogue and discussion, provide liturgical resources; promote networks

1. Primacy promoted as focus of unity
2. Work with the House of Bishops to define doctrine when necessary
3. Develop liturgical resources, sensitive to a multicultural context
4. Facilitate consultations regarding liturgy
5. Research theological/ethical issues to share with dioceses
6. Participate in the Anglican Consultative Council; fund to the extent possible
7. Foster and facilitate collaboration among Canadian theological colleges and between the national church and the colleges
8. Journey with indigenous peoples

Diocesan and Parish

Engage in theological/liturgical study and growth in understanding

1. Participate in theological and liturgical consultations
2. Contribute to the development of liturgical resources
3. Encourage use of liturgical resources
4. Encourage awareness of Canadian multicultural Anglican heritage

C. Nurture ecumenical relationships

National

Engage in ecumenical discussion and activity

1. Use the Lund Principle — work ecumenically wherever possible
2. Participate in the World Council of Churches and Canadian Council of Churches and fund to the extent possible
3. Engage in ecumenical/inter-faith dialogues

Diocesan and Parish

Engage in discussion and activity with ecumenical partners

1. Work ecumenically wherever possible
2. Engage in local dialogue with ecumenical and inter-faith participants

D. Advocate social justice and prophetic mission within Canada, especially in indigenous peoples' concerns and social, economic, and environmental justice issues

National

Concentrate on the promotion of networks and develop discussion frameworks; develop a new relationship with indigenous peoples

1. Build, facilitate, and animate networks in partnership with dioceses
2. Initiate development of frameworks to engage people in ethical reflection
3. Participate in ecumenically-based research, advocacy, and educational activities (i.e., through restructured coalitions)
4. Guide national/diocesan relationships using partnership principles
5. Develop targeted communications to enable better informed networks (e.g., downlinks, computer networks)
6. Journey with indigenous peoples toward healing, reconciliation, and self-determination

Parish and Diocesan

Participate in networks; build own programs

1. Participate in networks by entering into partnership, identifying participants, encouraging information flow, mobilizing around local concerns, supporting the work financially
2. Through the networks, join in advocacy to business and government
3. Participate in relationships with indigenous peoples

E. Affirm healing and reconciliation with Indigenous peoples *(Approved by General Synod 2001)*

National

Affirm healing and reconciliation with Indigenous peoples with increased resources to work toward:

1. Healing for those affected by the residential schools, their families, and their communities
2. Reconciliation within Canadian society of Aboriginal and non-Aboriginal people
3. Developing and enhancing the partnership of Aboriginal and non-Aboriginal Anglicans
4. Developing and enhancing the partnership of the Church with others working toward healing and reconciliation

F. Strengthen commitment of the whole Church to domestic mission in partnership with the Council of the North, and work with the Council of the North to move toward self-sufficiency

National

Co-ordinate transfer payments and encourage improvements in stewardship

1. Identify needs not currently being met
2. Encourage increased stewardship education in assisted dioceses
3. Continue to develop the Anglican Appeal partially for the support of the Council of the North

Diocesan and Parish

Support work in the North through apportionment grants and the Anglican Appeal

G. Provide services to dioceses — information, financial, administration

National

Provide and share expertise; co-ordinate communication

1. Provide communication services (research, resources, publishing, archives) to dioceses and to the national church to support the priorities
2. Affirm *The Journal*'s primary responsibility "... *to inform Anglicans in Canada about the domestic and international work of their church* ..." and the rest of the Sections 1–5 in the General Synod Handbook (App. C, pp. 149) within the context of a co-ordinated national communications approach. The independent editorial policy continues as so defined.
3. Facilitate networks of finance officers and financial development volunteers
4. Provide expertise and availability in pensions, administrative services, financial development, and gift planning
5. Develop proposals for a co-ordinated national fund-raising capability tailored to suit the needs of parishes, dioceses, and the national church, and focused on the priorities in this option
6. Develop a volunteer and staff resource capacity to assist dioceses in handling financial /legal/communications/personnel/property issues

Diocesan and Parish

Actively manage revenue; share information

1. Continue to collect money, manage gift planning programs, and contribute to apportionment and assessment budgets
2. Call on national skills and knowledge when needed
3. Participate in networks through their selected members
4. Provide news to share with the wider church
5. Increase attention to stewardship education

H. Eliminate other nationally co-ordinated domestic mission

National

No national program support

Eliminate all program development, resource production, consultation other than that required for the above (e.g., congregational development, youth ministry, stewardship education)

Diocesan and Parish

Develop and conduct programs as needed, e.g., congregational development, leadership training, and spiritual growth

Source: Internal document provided by the Office of the General Secretary of the Anglican Church of Canada

APPENDIX D
The Intensive/Interaction Workshop Method

The Intensive/Interaction Workshop Method is a qualitative technique of in-depth consultation, seeking human response to environmental conditions, behaviour, leisure, housing, culture, social services, etc. This method is premised on the assumption that for every identifiable situation there is a clear range of social response.

It assumes further that individuals in society can be held emotionally and intellectually responsible for both their own actions and those of their peers in explaining mass response to situations. Given these critical assumptions, individuals in a community are the base resource for information on a particular issue. Hence, the Intensive/Interaction Workshop Method was designed as a consultation tool.

To achieve its objective, it requires participants to be actively involved in thinking about issues.

In the group session, the moderator must, at all times, maintain a vital relationship with the group members, putting them at ease and allowing them to explore their own perceptions. This requires the moderator to be attuned to the language of the group and to relate to experiences that are meaningful to them. Through gentle probing, the moderator can encourage members of the group to think, in detail, about the problem and develop their responses thoughtfully.

From the groups as a whole, there will emerge a representation of the social context within which the individual makes decisions that result in action — which is, indeed, the "real world."

The Intensive/Interaction Workshop Method is

1. a tool for comfortable and actionable consultation
2. an evaluation tool, used to examine alternative aspects of issues and their impact on individuals
3. the relevance of these issues within the individual's broader context

Initial Stage

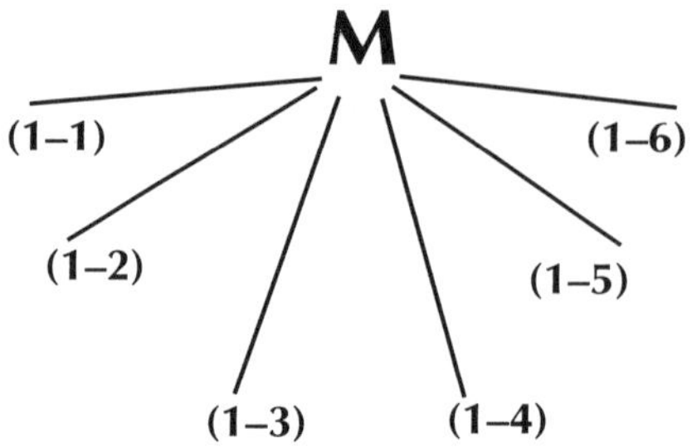

The relationship between the respondents is not yet formed. A one-to-one relationship between each respondent and the moderator begins to take shape.

Intermediate Stage

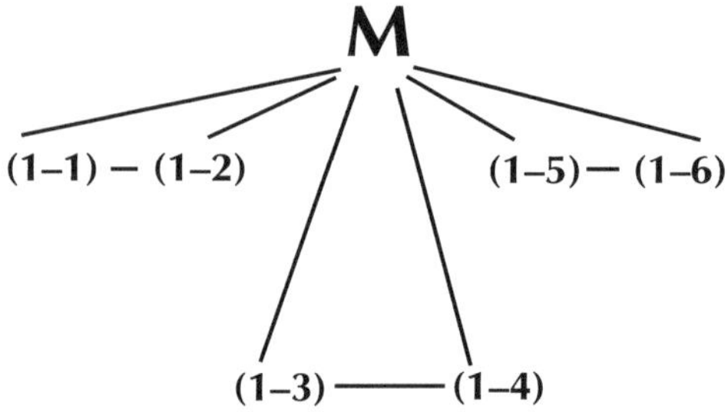

Tasks are used to allow respondents to develop a relationship and sense of *camaraderie* among themselves. Respondents are paired and given tasks to complete within a specified time. They must discuss among themselves, establish their individual positions and share them with each other. This focus on the assigned task allows each participant to collect their thoughts and thereby more clearly articulate their positions and viewpoints. This produces a clear view of both the range of opinion and the language the respondents use to express their ideas.

In subsequent tasks, composition of the pairs is changed. Two people do not work together more than once in the initial stages.

Concluding Stage

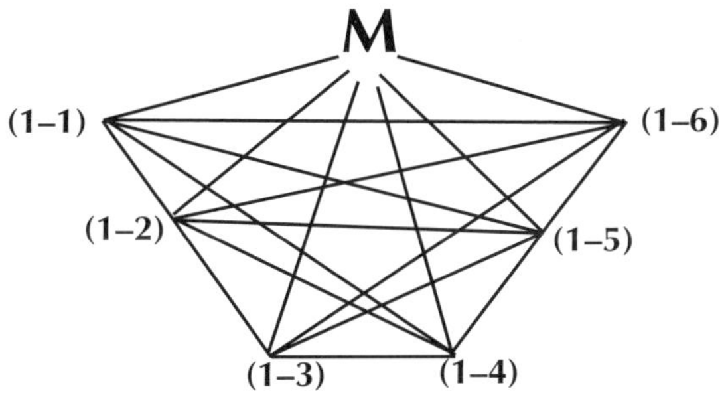

Each member of the group, by this stage, achieves some rapport and identification with other members of the group. Throughout this free exchange, people open themselves up to the group and areas of difference or similarities between individuals may be observed and assessed.

Sally Edmonds Preiner
Environics Research Group

APPENDIX E
The Book of Common Prayer and The Book of Alternative Services

LITURGY

At the heart of our spiritual lives

By Alyson Barnett-Cowan
Director, Faith, Worship and Ministry

For some time now, Canadian Anglicans have been living, sometimes comfortably, sometimes contentiously, with two major liturgical books. The *Book of Common Prayer* (1962) is the official, canonical book. The *Book of Alternative Services* (1985) was produced to provide alternatives to the language and style of the standard text, based on the insights of the ecumenical liturgical renewal movement; in many parishes the "alternative" has virtually replaced the BCP.

A BAS Evaluation Commission studied the theology and use of the BAS and made recommendations to the General Synod of 1995. Among other things, this commission proposed that some supplementary liturgical materials be prepared: new eucharistic prayers, some to reflect Reformed theological insights and some to be more inclusive in language and imagery, and Services of the Word for use in congregations where the eucharist cannot be the main service of the day. This material was prepared by the Faith, Worship and Ministry Committee, approved for trial use by the General Synod of 1998, and approved for use by the House of Bishops and the Council of General Synod (where approved by the Ordinary) in 2000.

In addition, Faith, Worship and Ministry prepared, tested, and brought forward for approval a service of Night Prayer (compline). These supplementary materials will be printed separately and together, and Night Prayer will be available on the web as soon as copyright permissions are secured.

The BAS Evaluation Commission also proposed that no decision about revision of either the BCP or the BAS be taken until at least 2001, the year in which the current mandate for the BAS expires.

Meanwhile, in many parishes alternatives to the alternative have been developed, and there are requests for various liturgies to supplement the existing books.

Some would like a version of the BCP liturgies that would, in contemporary English, convey its theology. Some would like liturgies that address God in ways that do not imply gender, or that have a wider range of images for God than presently appear. Some would like what are called seeker services: more flexible in format and open to a variety of contemporary language and style. Some would like an approved framework or template for Services of the Word, eucharist, baptism, marriage, and funerals that would enable local communities to develop culturally appropriate services, drawing on the many rich liturgical resources of the Anglican Communion and on ecumenical worship resources, or creating new resources.

At the same time, there is a strong concern that rites that are developed, and the theology expressed in them, have integrity and be congruent with Anglican tradition.

Knowing that the upcoming General Synod would have to make a decision at least about the future of the BAS, the Faith, Worship and Ministry Committee sponsored a series of liturgical consultations, one in each ecclesiastical province, in 2000.

These consultations brought together a wide range of participants, chosen by their dioceses, and they considered a wide range of questions relating to the future of liturgy. Participants reported a high level of energy and surprising consensus in the consultations. The strong view from all the consultations was that this is not the time to begin work on revision of either the *Book of Common Prayer* or the *Book of Alternative Services*, nor to attempt to produce one book. Instead, energy should be spent at regional and local levels on equipping people to lead liturgy well, producing resources to accompany existing books that meet local needs, translating liturgical texts into local languages, and considering the possibility of producing templates.

The Faith, Worship and Ministry Committee reviewed the recommendations and tested them with the House of Bishops and the Council of General Synod. As a result, the committee is bringing two resolutions to General Synod about liturgy:

1. that General Synod extend approval for the use of the *Book of Alternative Services* until such time as General Synod determines otherwise
2. that General Synod request the Faith, Worship and Ministry Committee to establish a process whereby regular regional liturgical forums can take place to address the recommendations made by the liturgical consultations of 2000

The Synod will have an opportunity in an information session to hear from participants in the liturgical consultations.

One of the recommendations from the liturgical consultations was that there be a "unifying common lectionary for the Anglican Church of Canada." After consideration of this proposal by the House of Bishops and the Council of General Synod, Faith, Worship and Ministry decided to ask the Council to ask the Anglican Book Centre to print future editions of the BAS with the Revised Common Lectionary instead of with the outdated lectionary that presently appears in the BAS. It is not proposed to change the lectionary printed in the BCP.

The 1995 General Synod asked that French translations of the BAS liturgies for baptism, eucharist, marriages, and funerals be prepared, especially for those situations in which congregations need to worship bilingually. Thanks to the dedicated work of a committee from the dioceses of Montreal, Ottawa, and Quebec, these texts are now ready and will be presented to the 2001 General Synod for approval.

Few subjects can animate Anglicans as easily as liturgy. Because our doctrinal heritage rests in part on a liturgical book (in its various editions), because liturgy is at the heart of our spiritual lives as individuals and as a community, debate about liturgy is debate about the core of our identity. The spirit in which this volatile issue was addressed by Anglicans from across the spectrum of theological and liturgical thought at the liturgical consultations bodes well for us as a community.

Respect, a desire to uphold both tradition and the new directions in which people are feeling called by the Spirit, a commitment to unity — these characteristics identified by participants may be the basis for a new way of approaching these questions together. It is in that spirit that we hope General Synod will meet to consider the future of liturgy in the Anglican Church of Canada.

*Ministry*Matters, Spring 2001
Published by the Information Resources Group of General Synod
Anglican Church of Canada

APPENDIX F
Residential Schools and the Anglican Church of Canada

ANGLICAN CHURCH OF CANADA'S APOLOGY TO NATIVE PEOPLE

A Message from the Primate to the National Native Convocation Minaki, Ontario

Friday, August 6, 1993

My Brothers and Sisters:

Together here with you I have listened as you have told your stories of the residential schools.

I have heard the voices that have spoken of pain and hurt experienced in the schools, and of the scars which endure to this day.

I have felt shame and humiliation as I have heard of suffering inflicted by my people, and as I think of the part our church played in that suffering.

I am deeply conscious of the sacredness of the stories that you have told and I hold in the highest honour those who have told them.

I have heard with admiration the stories of people and communities who have worked at healing, and I am aware of how much healing is needed.

I also know that I am in need of healing, and my own people are in need of healing, and our church is in need of healing. Without that healing, we will continue the same attitudes that have done such damage in the past.

I also know that healing takes a long time, both for people and for communities.

I also know that it is God who heals, and that God can begin to heal when we open ourselves, our wounds, our failures and our shame to God. I want to take one step along that path here and now.

I accept and I confess before God and you, our failures in the residential schools. We failed you. We failed ourselves. We failed God.

I am sorry, more than I can say, that we were part of a system which took you and your children from home and family.

I am sorry, more than I can say, that we tried to remake you in our image, taking from you your language and the signs of your identity.

I am sorry, more than I can say, that in our schools so many were abused physically, sexually, culturally and emotionally.

On behalf of the Anglican Church of Canada, I present our apology.

I do this at the desire of those in the Church like the National Executive Council, who know some of your stories and have asked me to apologize.

I do this in the name of many who do not know these stories.

And I do this even though there are those in the church who cannot accept the fact that these things were done in our name.

As soon as I am home, I shall tell all the bishops what I have said, and ask them to co-operate with me and with the National Executive Council in helping this healing at the local level. Some bishops have already begun this work.

I know how often you have heard words which have been empty because they have not been accompanied by actions. I pledge to you my best efforts, and the efforts of our church at the national level, to walk with you along the path of God's healing.

The work of the Residential Schools Working Group, the video, the commitment and the effort of the Special Assistants to the Primate for this work, the grants available for healing conferences, are some signs of that pledge, and we shall work for others.

This is Friday, the day of Jesus' suffering and death. It is the anniversary of the first atomic bomb at Hiroshima, one of the most terrible injuries ever inflicted by one people on another.

But even atomic bombs and Good Friday are not the last word. God raised Jesus from the dead as a sign that life and wholeness are the everlasting and unquenchable purpose of God.

Thank you for listening to me.

+ Michael, Archbishop and Primate

Source: www.anglican.ca/ministry/rs/resources/apology.html

RESPONSE TO THE PRIMATE AT THE NATIONAL NATIVE CONVOCATION

Delivered by Vi Smith on behalf of the elders and participants Minaki, Ontario

Saturday, August 7, 1993

On behalf of this gathering, we acknowledge and accept the apology that the Primate has offered on behalf of the Anglican Church of Canada.

It was offered from his heart with sincerity, sensitivity, compassion and humility. We receive it in the same manner. We offer praise and thanks to our Creator for his courage.

We know it wasn't easy. Let us keep him in our hearts and prayers, that God will continue to give him the strength and courage to continue with his tasks.

Source: www.anglican.ca/ministry/rs/resources/apology.html

PASTORAL LETTER FROM ARCHBISHOP MICHAEL PEERS

May 28, 2000

Dear Brothers and Sisters in Christ:

I write to share something of this moment in the life of the Anglican Church of Canada. In this troubling time we are faced with litigation so costly as to change radically our structures and our life as a national church. But the time is also profoundly hopeful; God leads us ever deeper into the path of healing and new life.

Simply put: resulting from abuse in the residential schools, there are over 1,600 claims of varying kinds brought against the General Synod of the Anglican Church of Canada.

About one hundred cases involve the proven abuse of children, and the perpetrators are in prison. The costs of litigation and settlements for these alone is sufficient to exhaust all the assets of the General Synod and of some dioceses involved.

What does this mean? For the national church, the way we presently carry out our mission will be modified. We are negotiating with the federal government in order to find alternatives to litigation by which we can make a just contribution to compensation. We will know in a few months if an agreement is possible. However, whether or not this is achievable, we will be a very different Church.

Where in this do I discern hope? At the heart of it, we trust God is with us in the choices we face, that we will find new ways to carry out our shared mission and that we will continue to work for healing and reconciliation. Healing and reconciliation is our first and clearly affirmed goal. Both the Council of General Synod and the House of Bishops gave it the strongest possible support in meetings earlier this month. The legacy of the schools has been deeply wounding. Healing never happens if we ignore the wounds. The first step is truth-telling — recognizing and acknowledging past failures. The Anglican Church of Canada collaborated with the Government of Canada in a policy that brought pain to many individuals and despair in many communities. That injury continues into the present. We have an obligation, and a will born of our desire to be just, to account for past injustice.

Healing also requires being prepared to turn and walk in a different direction. Indeed repentance means "turning around." The wounds of past prejudices, injustices and broken trust will never be healed unless we "strive for justice and peace among all people, and respect the dignity of every human being." Ever since the General Synod of 1969 set us in a new direction, aboriginal and non-aboriginal Anglicans have been learning to walk together in a different way. I assure aboriginal brothers and sisters that we will not be deflected from this road. I call each of us to recommit ourselves to that path, so that together we may find the healing Christ offers in his Cross and Resurrection.

I want to assure all Anglicans that what is at risk financially are our assets, not the contributions that provide for the ongoing ministry and mission of the church at parish, diocesan or national levels. Your contributions serve the mission of the church — not the costs of litigation. If our present structures cease to exist, we will find a way for our contributions to continue to serve that work.

How do we continue authentically if the depletion of our assets means we are unable to meet the claims against us? I believe that our greatest asset in the Anglican Church of Canada is our ability to be in relationship, to support and care for each other. This will survive. So will our capacity to worship, to learn, to grow, to serve and to bear witness to Christ. Nothing at the heart of our faith — our desire for wholeness and healing in ourselves, in our relationships, in our country and in our world — is at risk. We have these abundant and enduring assets that will help us continue to do justice and work for healing.

As we move into the future, I ask for your prayers: for the bishops and people of Cariboo and Qu'Appelle dioceses who are most immediately concerned; for members of the Anglican Council of Indigenous Peoples who give outstanding leadership, and who bear such love for the whole of the Church; for those whose ministries are given over to witness in the courts.

Pray that we may all perceive the need for our own healing.

We read in the gospels how Jesus speaks of things ending — of the heavens and earth in turmoil. In one sense, it is a picture of chaos. But Jesus says that it is more truly to be interpreted as a birth: "...when these things begin to take place, stand up and raise your heads, because your redemption is drawing near." (Luke 21:28) For many in the church, things are being shaken, and it feels like chaos. But we stand up and raise our heads; God is present and leads us into something new.

When we look up at the evening horizon, we see the sun falling. Turn the other way, and we will see it rise. I believe with all my heart, and with sure confidence, that God is with us both in the falling and in the rising, and that, even in our dying, God will bring us to new life.

+ *Michael, Archbishop and Primate*

http://anglican.ca/news/ans/ans.html?ansItem=2000-05-28_a.ans

BACKGROUND INFORMATION ON RESIDENTIAL SCHOOLS

Office of the General Secretary
Anglican Church of Canada

August 30, 2000

Concern for justice

Abuses were real and people were harmed.

- The most obvious harm arises from the sexual abuse, or by extreme physical abuse. In some cases sexual abuse has been established by a criminal conviction, beyond a reasonable doubt.
- More broadly, in many schools, the suppression of native culture and languages produced harmful effects.
- At the same time, the schools, which were regulated and funded by the government, were consistently run 'on the cheap,' without adequate funding; many children were not properly fed or nourished.
- More broadly still, the policy of assimilation of which the schools were a major instrument — along with other government policies such as the *Indian Act* — harmed native communities beyond the residential schools and continue to harm communities today.

All the above are named as causes of action in suits against Canada and church organizations.

However, only 'recognized' causes of action — physical and sexual abuse, and failure to provide the necessities of life — are being dealt with in litigation and alternative dispute resolution (ADR) processes at this time, according to government policy.

Continuing injustice and perceived injustice prevents reconciliation.

Litigation and ADR models now underway will take several years to run their course, although many plaintiffs are very elderly.

- They will not address the largest categories of abuses above, particularly the claims of cultural and inter-generational abuse. As a result, they are likely to increase the ill-will between Aboriginal and non-Aboriginal Canadians.

We share with the Law Commission of Canada a concern to identify redress models that will better meet the needs of Aboriginal Canadians.

The Commission did not feel any single approach should be adopted exclusively, but it did conclude "that redress programs are the official response that can be most effectively designed to meet the complete range of goals that have been identified...."

> "What are the needs of survivors? They are as diverse and unique as survivors themselves. Nevertheless, the Commission was able to identify certain recurring themes in the manner these needs were expressed. Survivors seek: an acknowledgement of the harm done and accountability for that harm; an apology; access to therapy and to education; financial compensation; some means of memorialising the experiences of children in institutions; and a commitment to raising public awareness of institutional child abuse and preventing its recurrence."
> [The Law Commission report, *Restoring Dignity: Responding to Abuse in Canadian Institutions*, is available at www.lcc.gc.ca]

Our goals in relation to residential schools:

- *to contribute to healing and reconciliation with Indigenous peoples*
- *to survive* (so that we may continue our mission, including our work in healing and reconciliation)
- *to reach an agreement with the Government of Canada* (so that we can survive)

Healing and reconciliation

Our understanding of healing and reconciliation encompasses the need for all of us, Anglicans and all Canadians, to address the forces within our social structures and ourselves that perpetuate injustice and discrimination. It is enriched by the understanding shared by Aboriginal members: For the Cree, the meaning of healing and reconciliation is this: to be purified and made whole so that nothing is lacking in you, and relationships are at peace. To the Lakota it means nothing blocking health and life so that one can walk a straight road. To the Inuit it means taking a burden off your chest. And to the Siksika it means letting go and lifting off burdens so one may rest before moving on.[1]

So far, our journey toward healing has included:

- promoting awareness and education among the non-Aboriginal population (for example, the work of our Indigenous Justice Coordinator; the *Ministry*Matters special issue, *Residential Schools: Legacy and Hope;* the special section of the May 2000 *Anglican Journal*)
- the Apology which Archbishop Michael Peers gave on behalf of our church in August 1993
- journeying with Aboriginal members in their exploration of a Covenant (see box)
- the diverse initiatives supported by our healing fund
- the vision and program of healing in the Diocese of Keewatin, which has launched a multi-year program dedicated to education, training, prevention and healing, ultimately to ensure that the church is a safe place where all can walk together without fear, guilt or blame
- our church's engagement and support over four decades with issues of justice for Aboriginal persons, particularly our support for land claims and self-determination

A Covenant

We, representatives of the Indigenous people of the Anglican Church of Canada, meeting in Winnipeg from the 23 to 26 of April, 1994, pledge ourselves to this covenant for the sake of our people and in trust of our Lord and Saviour, Jesus Christ:

Under the guidance of God's spirit we agree to do all we can to call our people into unity in a new, self determining community within the Angican Church of Canada.

To this end, we extend the hand of partnership to all those who will help us build a truly Anglican Indigenous Church in canada.

May God bless this new vision and give us grace to accomplish it.

Our structure

- The General Synod is the church's national body. It was created in 1893 by a group of dioceses (and larger regional structures known as

1 The Rev. Mervyn Wolfleg, presentation to the Council of General Synod, May 2000

'ecclesiastical provinces') in order to carry out certain functions on a national basis. Chief among these are mission in Canada and mission overseas. Mission involves spreading the good news of God's love through Jesus Christ, by word and deed. Missionaries were the primary agents of mission through most of the 19th Century and the earlier part of the 20th. In recent times, both overseas and at home, mission has been characterized by working in partnership with the local community and responding to its expressed needs.
- The Canadian Church is made up of 29 dioceses, each led by a bishop. Each diocese is independently incorporated and functions autonomously.
- More than 700,000 Anglicans are enrolled as members in one of about 1,800 local parishes across Canada.

Our financial assets

- The General Synod annually solicits funds from its dioceses to support the national program, and these voluntary contributions — which ultimately originate with individual Anglicans — are the General Synod's primary source of revenue.
- Our annual budget is approximately $11 million.
- Over many years, additional funds, such as bequests, have established modest reserves, which in 1999 produced income from investments of $370,000.
- The General Synod owns only one property, an office building in Toronto worth between $3 million and $4 million.
- General Synod operates a book and religious supply store with 1999 inventory valued at approximately $1.5 million.
- All told, the total assets of General Synod amount to less than $10 million (and perhaps considerably less in a liquidation).

These are the only assets available to settle claims against General Synod. The General Synod does not own local churches, any more than the federal government owns municipal buildings.

Scope of the lawsuits

- Approximately 7,000 individual plaintiffs are suing the government of Canada at August 2000. Claims continue to increase.
- Approximately 1,600 of these claims directly or indirectly involve the General Synod.

- Most General Synod lawsuits also involve a diocese, particularly British Columbia, Cariboo, Calgary, Saskatchewan, Qu'Appelle, Brandon, Keewatin, and Huron.
- In many cases, plaintiffs have chosen not to sue the church. The church is involved because of cross-claims or third-party claims lodged by the government.
- At the present time, General Synod is in court in British Columbia in actions involving eight plaintiffs. *Only one of those plaintiffs has sued the church. The government has named the church as a third party in the case of the other seven.*

Claims and legal costs

- The General Synod is named (either by a plaintiff or the government) in approximately 360 cases, including three class action suits. The damages claimed in these suits exceed $2 billion.
- Estimates of the government's ultimate liability for residential schools claims range from $1 billion to $5 billion.
- Legal costs continue to escalate.

What we offer to meet the needs of the residential school survivors, as identified by the Law Commission of Canada

- We have acknowledged harm and offered apology, and we can continue to be present in forums where acknowledgement is made and apology offered. We bring to this task a long-term commitment, engagement and expertise in working at healing and reconciliation.
- We can participate in financial compensation to the extent of our capacity. This includes limited current assets, and the potential to raise funds for healing and reconciliation into the future.
- We can help to memorialize the experiences.
- We have assisted in raising awareness of abuse and taken steps to prevent its recurrence, and we can continue to do so.

Additionally we can contribute to healing from our experiences of

- long-standing partnership with Indigenous peoples and supportive engagement with issues of Indigenous justice
- continuing ministry in 225 Indigenous communities, including the ministry of four Indigenous bishops and more than 100 Indigenous priests and deacons

- extensive involvement with Northern communities, including direct contributions of $2.7 million annually (about a quarter of our national budget)

To Canadian society generally, we offer

- opportunities for spiritual nurture and guidance
- direct provision of hundreds of social services in thousands of Canadian communities
- major support (both time and money) for non-religious charitable activities (increasingly important as government cutbacks require greater reliance on volunteers)
- as a national organization, we contribute to social cohesion and stability
- our mission and development work enhances positive images of Canada abroad

Some of these contributions are provided through the General Synod; some through dioceses and local parishes; many through the good will and commitment of individual Anglicans. Although a General Synod bankruptcy would not prevent all this work from continuing, the disruption would be severe enough to have negative impacts across the board.

Need for urgent attention

- If the Department of Justice continues its approach to litigation, our resources will soon be exhausted, leading to bankruptcy
- This would massively disrupt our ability to participate in healing and reconciliation.
- Our capacity as a national organization would be significantly diminished.
- We fear the possibility of a backlash — not necessarily from Anglicans — against Native peoples if they are perceived as contributing to the bankruptcy of a church organization. This would have a negative impact on Canada.

Remember…

The 200 years of Anglican missionary service has blossomed into the full membership and fellowship of Indigenous Canadians within the Anglican Church. This is a valuable national asset for Canada that should be sustained and reinforced, not destroyed.

For further information

Residential Schools: Legacy and Hope (*Ministry*Matters Special Edition, Winter 2000)
Sins of the Fathers (*Anglican Journal* Special Issue, May 2000)
Restoring Dignity: Responding to Abuse in Canadian Institutions, report of the Law Commission of Canada
Residential School Updates by Archdeacon Jim Boyles (periodic)
All the above, and many other resources, are available through our web site at *www.anglican.ca/ministry/rs*

Material above extracted from documents posted at: www.anglican.ca/ministry/rs

APPENDIX G
Position Papers: The House of Bishops on Homosexuality

SOURCE: ANS / 1997 OCTOBER 30 / PRESS RELEASE

Human Sexuality: A Statement by the Anglican Bishops of Canada — 1997

TEXT: MISSISSAUGA, Ont. (Oct. 30, 1997) — Canada's Anglican bishops, meeting here this week, approved the following statement which updates their 1979 guidelines dealing with the ordination of homosexual persons and pastoral relationship with the homosexual community.

The statement was drafted by a task force and adopted with near unanimity, without change.

- 30 -

Human sexuality: A statement by the Anglican Bishops of Canada — 1997

The Background

In 1976 the House of Bishops of the Anglican Church of Canada sought advice as it faced the issue of homosexuality in contemporary society and how the church ought to relate pastorally, and in terms of ordination. A task force presented a lengthy report to the bishops.

By 1979 the bishops had committed themselves to further study and they requested the preparation of study materials to help further discussion at all levels of the church. These materials were published in 1985.

In 1979, as an interim measure, the bishops issued a statement based on the following belief: We believe as Christians, that homosexual persons, as children of God, have a full and equal claim with all other persons, upon the love, acceptance, concern and pastoral care of the Church.

As well, the Bishops issued a four point pastoral guideline for themselves as they considered the admission of individual persons to the church's ordained ministry.

1. Our present and future considerations about homosexuality should be pursued within the larger study of human sexuality in its totality.
2. We accept all persons, regardless of sexual orientation, as equal before God; our acceptance of persons with homosexual orientation is not an acceptance of homosexual activity.
3. We do not accept the blessing of homosexual unions.
4. We will not call into question the ordination of a person who has shared with the bishop his/her homosexual orientation if there has been a commitment to the Bishop to abstain from sexual acts with persons of the same sex as part of the requirement for ordination.

In referring to this guideline in the press, Archbishop Scott, Primate of the Anglican Church of Canada at that time said, Our statement is not meant to be, in any way, legislation or a final doctrinal statement. It is a pastoral statement and we intend it to assist us in the exercise of our pastoral ministry within the Church.

The house held a number of study sessions on the topic of human sexuality through the 1980s. In 1991 a new task force was constituted by the Primate.

At the General Synod of 1992 a major block of time was devoted to an open forum on the topic. More materials were made available for study and by 1994/95 approximately 170 groups and 2,500 people had used the study guide "Hearing Diverse Voices, Seeking Common Ground."

At the 1995 General Synod, an important report was presented, following a hearing, which lead to a motion being presented and strongly supported which:

Affirmed the presence and contributions of gay men and lesbians in the life of the church and condemned bigotry, violence and hatred directed toward any due to their sexual orientation.

This report recommended among other things, that the process of dialogue continue; that all of us should, "learn and reflect more about our sexuality as a whole," and that the dialogue should be extended so that the, "whole church family has an opportunity to be involved".

The Faith Worship and Ministry Committee of the ACC was given a mandate to provide leadership to the church to ensure a continuation of the dialogue.

All of this effort has fostered a greater understanding of what it is to be a gay man or lesbian in the church and a heightened sense of pastoral concern on the part of the church. Also, as gay men and lesbians have found greater acceptance in the church, they have been enabled to share their experiences in a more public way to the benefit of the whole church which has become increasingly aware of the breadth and depth of their contribution.

At its April 1997 meeting, discussing this topic for the first time in open session, the House of Bishops continued its deliberations and requested the task force to redraft the 1979 guideline in the light of new pastoral awareness while at the same time retaining the original intent of the guideline. In undertaking this task we seek to articulate how far we have come, as well as to acknowledge those areas where continued study and dialogue is necessary.

Theological reflection and pastoral action in the Church since 1979 have focused on four key areas, and it is these that shape our considerations in this statement. The church has reflected on the place of gay and lesbian persons in society; the place of gay and lesbian persons in the church; the significance of committed sexually active relationships between people of the same sex and the significance of such relationships for ordination of gay and lesbian persons.

Gay and Lesbian Persons in Society

As Christians we believe that homosexual persons are created in the image and likeness of God and have a full and equal claim with all other persons upon the love, acceptance, concern and care of the church. As an expression of this love and care, the gospel of Jesus Christ compels Christians to oppose all forms of human injustice and to affirm that all persons are brothers and sisters for whom Christ died.

It is on the basis of these theological insights, which remain pertinent irrespective of any considerations of the appropriateness or otherwise of homosexual acts, that the Anglican Church of Canada has affirmed that gay and lesbian persons are entitled to equal protection under the law with all other Canadian citizens. Thus, this House supported the passage of bill C-33 that made sexual orientation a prohibited ground for discrimination under the Canadian Charter of Human Rights and Freedoms. We call upon the church and all its members to continue to work to safeguard the freedom, dignity and responsibility of every person and to seek an end to discrimination.

Gay and Lesbian Persons in the Church

We are thankful to see a new sensitivity emerging towards gay and lesbian persons in the Church. No longer can we talk in the abstract. We are experiencing a growing awareness that the persons of whom we speak are among us. They are our sons and daughters. They are our friends and relatives. This recognition has not always been present. The story of the Church's attitude to gay and lesbian people has too often been one of standing at a distance, even of prejudice, ignorance and oppression. All of us need to acknowledge this, and to repent for any part we may have had in creating it.

In our baptism we covenant to seek and to serve Christ in all persons. We now call the church to reaffirm the mutuality of that covenant, a covenant that encourages and enables us to love others as Christ loves us. This covenant will no longer allow us to regard those among us whose orientation is homosexual simply as "needy objects" for pastoral care. Instead we are partners, celebrating together the dignity of every human being, and reaching out together for the wholeness offered to us in the Gospel.

The church affirms its traditional teaching that only the sexual union of male and female can find appropriate expression within the covenant of Holy Matrimony. However, we recognize that some homosexuals live in committed sexual relationships for mutual support, help and comfort. We wish to continue open and respectful dialogue with those who sincerely believe that sexuality expressed within a committed homosexual relationship is God's call to them, and we affirm our common desire to seek together the fullness of life revealed in Christ.

Blessing of Covenanted Relationships

We continue to believe that committed same sex relationships should not be confused with Holy Matrimony. The house will not authorize any act that appears to promote this confusion. There is, and needs to be, ongoing discussion about how to respond appropriately to faithful and committed same sex relationships. In the context of the ongoing debate this would necessitate respectful listening and learning about the nature of such relationships and their meaning for the persons involved in them. We recognize that relationships of mutual support, help and comfort between homosexual persons exist and are to be preferred to relationships that are anonymous and transient. We disagree among ourselves about whether such relationships can be expressions of God's will and purpose.

While consensus may be unlikely in the near future, we believe that study and dialogue continue to be fruitful. As we continue to listen together to scripture, tradition, and reasoned argument based on the experience of the Church, including and especially the experience of its gay and lesbian members, we grow in our recognition that our disagreements reflect our attempts to be faithful to the Gospel in our different personal and pastoral contexts.

As long as such dialogue continues to be fruitful we believe it should continue. We are not ready to authorize the blessing of relationships between persons of the same sex. However, in interpreting the Gospel, we must always reflect on the context to which it is addressed. We are, therefore, committed to ongoing study of human sexuality and of the nature and characteristics of human intimacy and family life as it exists in our society.

Ordination of Gay and Lesbian Persons

Among our clergy there are some who are gay or lesbian. Their ministries are often highly dedicated and greatly blessed. God has endowed them with many intellectual and spiritual gifts and we give thanks for their ministries. We reaffirm that sexual orientation in and of itself is not a barrier to ordination or the practice of ministry within the church. Within the wider parameters of suitability, it is the manner in which sexuality is expressed that must be considered. Our intimate relationships are an expression of the most profound possibilities for human relationships, including our relationship with God (Eph.5:32). At ordination, candidates promise to live their lives and shape their relationships so as to provide a "wholesome example" to the people of God (BCP, 642). Exemplary behaviour for persons who are not married includes a commitment to remain chaste.

Conclusion

Our discussions over the past few years have taught us much. We do not have a common mind on all things. We see in part and we know in part. Where we disagree we need to continue to read the scriptures together and to engage in dialogue, that we might listen for what the Spirit is saying to the Church today.

APPENDIX H
Debate on Same-Sex Unions in the Diocese of New Westminster, BC

MOTION PASSED AT THE SYNOD OF THE DIOCESE OF NEW WESTMINSTER, MAY 1998

BE IT RESOLVED THAT the Synod of the Diocese of New Westminster asks the Bishop to authorize clergy in this diocese to bless covenanted same-sex unions, subject to such conditions as the Bishop deems appropriate.

Source: http://www.vancouver.anglican.ca

Bishop's Announcement on the Blessing of Same-Sex Unions

The following is a copy of the statement made by Bishop Michael Ingham to the Clergy and Lay Delegates to Synod of the Diocese of New Westminster in Christ Church Cathedral, Vancouver, on Saturday, January 16, 1999.

In Response to Motion 9 of the Synod of the Diocese of New Westminster May 1998

A Statement by Bishop Michael Ingham

Let me begin by thanking all those who have sent messages of encouragement over the last few weeks. I have received cards, letters and phone calls from people across the diocese and all across Canada assuring me of support and prayer at this important time. To each of you I am very grateful.

I must also express my thanks to the members of the Council of Advice. We spent many hours listening to each other and to the different voices of the church. We did so in a spirit of mutual respect. We did so with concern for homosexual men and women who are embers of our church, a concern we shared across our divergent theologies. Our meetings were centred around the celebration of the Eucharist. And I believe the Holy Spirit was with us as we listened for God's direction.

In the last few weeks, many people have told me they would support the decision whatever it is. This has been deeply encouraging to me. It shows there is a strong constituency among Anglicans which can rise above partisan spirit and defensiveness. I commend this selfless generosity to every member of our church. If we are to move forward together on this issue, we will need a deep loyalty to our Lord, and a willingness to put private opinion aside for the sake of each other.

The Context of the Synod Vote

The blessing of same-sex unions is a complex issue, and it is a disputed issue. It is something on which Christians can in good conscience disagree. People of differing convictions, acting in good faith, justify their position on the basis of the Gospel and church tradition as they understand it. Each feels they are acting on the basis of love for homosexual people themselves. Those who oppose the blessing of unions believe they must do so in obedience to the Bible and the history of Christian teaching. Those who favour change in this area believe it is time to accept modern understandings of human sexuality, and of the Bible, and that it is time to bring an end to discrimination in the church based on sexual orientation.

Homosexuality and same-sex unions have been under discussion in the Anglican Church of Canada for more than twenty years. The first House of Bishops Guidelines were published in 1979. The "Report On Human Sexuality" was authorized by the National Executive Council in 1986. It was widely read and provoked intense discussion across this country. The General Synod held its first open Forum on Homosexuality in Toronto in 1992, and the second one was televised live back here to Vancouver from Ottawa in 1995. Every parish in our diocese was given the opportunity to participate in a national study on homosexuality called "Hearing Diverse Voices" from 1994 to 1995, and many parishes did so.

Homosexuality has been under discussion within the diocese for more than ten years. Our diocesan Synods have had motions on the subject of one sort or another since 1989. In 1995 Synod asked me to establish a Task Force on Human Sexuality which worked for two years to produce resources for parish discussion. Two public forums were held in different parts of the diocese to discuss scriptural, doctrinal and ethical questions. In 1997 we had an open Day of Dialogue on Homosexuality to which several hundred people came.

Our debate last May took place against this considerable background. Members of Synod had been elected in the normal way by their parishes. They were chosen for their wisdom and ability, and not for their position on any single issue. The Synod was probably as representative a body as we could assemble in New Westminster. Our debate was characterized by a deep attentiveness to one another, by passionate commitment to the Gospel differently understood, and by a spirit of charity and mutual respect. You remember that we took the vote after a time of prayer, and by secret ballot. There was no coercion. It was a free vote, and the outcome was a narrow margin of support.

In the months afterwards it became clear that many in the diocese welcomed the decision, and many did not. For some it was the fulfilling of years of prayer that the church might one day fully accept gay and lesbian relationships. For others the Synod vote prompted preparations to leave the Anglican Church altogether. There were threats to plunge the diocese into litigation. Some felt pushed to the edge because of their commitment to tradition. There were angry comments, sometimes unfair and personal in nature, as people vented their feelings of loss.

At the same time, a number people came back to church after hearing of our decision in the media. There was new interest and enthusiasm in some of our parishes. Members of other dioceses looked to New Westminster with a sense of hope, glad that there had been a breakthrough in the discussion in Canada. All these reactions are normal and understandable. Changes in tradition always provoke divergent responses.

Following our Synod, the national House of Bishops took up the subject again, and so did the Lambeth Conference. The House of Bishops in November restated its opposition to the blessing of same-sex unions and said it would be inappropriate for a bishop and a diocese to authorize them. The Lambeth Conference, after a heated and rather sordid debate last summer, said it "cannot advise" the blessing of same-sex unions. It found homosexuality to be "incompatible with Scripture," though at the same time it called for the church to listen to the voices of gay and lesbian Christians.

We are not alone, therefore, in trying to discern the will of God in this matter. Homosexuality is under debate throughout the world in almost every part of the church. There have been equally difficult and controversial issues in Christian history before now. No generation is spared the struggle of interpreting the Gospel in each new era. This always involves making decisions about whether to maintain the tradition unchanged, or whether to adapt to new insights and learning. Anglicanism has proven itself to be very skilled in finding the right balance between conservation and progress. I have no doubt we will do so on this question too.

Questions Raised by Motion 9

In the large volume of correspondence which has come in over the last eight months, a number of questions were raised about Motion 9 and its meaning. Some of them were put forward during the debate itself in May, and were sent in again because they were not answered in the debate. The questions can be classified roughly into three groups.

One had to do with doctrinal, scriptural and ethical issues. What is meant by 'blessing'? What is meant by 'unions'? Is it clear what we are talking about? Is the blessing of same-sex unions the same thing as marriage? Some wanted to see how same-sex unions could be justified on the basis of Scripture, and asked if modern biblical scholarship could provide a rationale for this. Others wanted to see a more comprehensive statement of human sexuality as a whole and how homosexual relationships are to be understood within Christian sexual ethics.

A second group of questions was about pastoral and liturgical issues. What would a ceremony in church look like? What would be required of its participants? What preparation should be necessary, and who should be accepted, whom refused? Some people were uncertain whether or not they could agree to the blessing of unions without an actual text before them of what is being proposed. Others wondered what long-term support the church is prepared to offer people who enter into these vows and commitments.

A third group of questions had to do with legal and canonical issues. It was argued that the diocese lacks the authority to proceed by itself in such a matter. A case was made that we would be in violation of the Solemn Declaration of 1893, the Thirty-Nine Articles, and the Canons of General Synod. It was also said that, since Motion 9 involves doctrine, the vote in May should have been taken by orders, clergy and laity voting separately.

All these questions and concerns were taken very seriously. I have done my best to listen to the voices of the church, both within the diocese and beyond. Many of these voices represent an honest search for clarification and understanding of what the Synod had done or intended would be done. It is clear from the correspondence and from other reactions that not everyone in the diocese has had an opportunity to think through the issues entailed in Motion 9.

Although there has been dialogue on this subject for years within the church, dialogue in many of our parishes only began after Motion 9 was passed.

Factors Leading To My Decision

In trying to determine how I should respond to Motion 9 I have struggled with a number of factors.

One is the presence in our church of gay and lesbian persons. They are baptized and communicant members within the Body of Christ and deserve the same respect, the same pastoral and sacramental care, as everyone else. It is a constant wonder to me that gay and lesbian Christians have kept faith with the church these many years, despite the church's unwillingness to affirm their relationships, their commitments, their love. They have suffered rejection in both church and society. I think our Synod in 1998 took the decision it did from a desire to end discrimination against our fellow members in the Body of Christ, and that it did so believing this to be the will of God.

A second factor, however, is the position of the House of Bishops and the Lambeth Conference. These two bodies are clearly asking us to wait. There is a strong instinct among Anglicans to balance the sometimes conflicting imperatives of unity and diversity. We wish to be faithful to God and also to the church to which we belong. And it is clear that any action we take will have an impact on other members of the church, at least in Canada.

Canadian bishops have in the past been quite tolerant of diversity in a number of controversial areas, and often supportive of what is today called the local option. This has been true even in matters involving doctrine. But there is strong resistance among the present House to any local option with respect to homosexuality.

Nevertheless, neither the House of Bishops nor the Lambeth Conference is legislative. Neither has the power to compel compliance by this or any other diocese. In fact, since the Lambeth Conference it has become clear that compliance on this issue is far from uniform. 185 bishops from around the world, including nine Primates, have signed a statement pledging to work for the full inclusion of gay and lesbian people in the life of the church.

Several dioceses in the Episcopal Church of the United States have opted to continue ordinations and blessings contrary to the Lambeth position. In this country more and more parishes are choosing to become "affirming" congregations, meaning open and welcoming to gay and lesbian people as singles, couples or families. But the fact remains that the majority of bishops, in Canada and throughout the world, are opposed to partnerships between people of the same sex.

A third factor in my decision is that our whole church is in a process of change on this subject. Change happens slowly, and it happens step by step. Canadian Roman Catholic scholar Gregory Baum has said that the church first begins to change its mind when it senses that some doctrine or tradition violates the primacy of love.

When beliefs which were formerly accepted no longer meet the test of justice or compassion, the church begins a re-examination of its Scripture and doctrine. This is a slow process, but a necessary one, because Christians must be convinced that any change to tradition is a development of faith and not a repudiation of it.

Many Anglicans, and many others, appear to be changing their minds on this matter, but they need to know that in doing so they will remain faithful to the high ideals and truths of our heritage, and not engaging in mere imitation of the secular culture in which we live. As I have come to my decision, therefore, I have tried to find a way of proceeding by evolution rather than by revolution.

Related to this is a fourth factor. As a bishop I am conscious of my responsibility to guard the unity of the church. Change is achieved when the "mind of the faithful" — the "sensus fidelium" — is ready to accept a new practice or belief. The consensus of the faithful does not have to be universal or unanimous for change to happen locally. That is, we don't need to have the agreement of everyone everywhere. But it would need to have the strong support of the local church, that is, the diocese. If the Diocese of New Westminster wishes to move in the direction of change on same-sex unions a substantial consensus would be necessary to proceed.

My Decision on Motion 9

The decision I am announcing today is an attempt to balance these factors and to help find a way forward in this complex matter. I am of the view that neither a "yes" nor a "no" would be a satisfactory resolution to our discussions at this time. Even a qualified "yes" or a qualified "no" would be equally unsatisfactory because both would have the same effect, that is, to end the dialogue that has been started by Motion 9. My decision is in six parts. Each is inter-connected with the others, and it follows now.

1. Diocese To Vote Again

I will ask the diocese to vote again on Motion 9 in two years' time, to see if it wishes to confirm the decision of 1998. That will be at the regular Synod in 2001. Until that time, we shall maintain the status quo with respect to same-sex unions, out of consideration for the House of Bishops, Lambeth, and those members of our diocese for whom this is still a matter of conscientious difficulty.

2. Parishes Twinned For Dialogue

I shall request each parish, and every member of the diocese, to engage in a process of intentional dialogue on same-sex unions during these next two years. To this end, I will establish a system of "parish twinning." Each parish will be linked with another in a process of learning, listening and study. The diocese will provide training and support to parish leaders, and study resources for the dialogue.

3. Bishop's Commission on Gay and Lesbian Voices

In response to the Lambeth Conference, I shall establish a Bishop's Commission on Gay and Lesbian Voices. This Commission will consist of representatives of the gay and lesbian community along with others. Its mandate will be to assist the parishes in hearing the voice and experience of gay and lesbian Christians. It will play a vital role in the dialogue process, and I expect every twinned parish to invite them and to hear from them.

4. Commission on Faith and Doctrine

I shall establish a Commission on Faith and Doctrine whose mandate will be to help parishes listen to the voice of Scripture and church teaching, both with the ears of tradition and with the insights of modern biblical and theological scholarship. This Commission will provide short study papers discussing the doctrinal and ethical issues raised by same-sex unions. I shall refer to them a number of specific questions for response. Their work will provide the basic written material for study and dialogue.

5. Canonical and Legal Commission

I shall establish a Commission on Legal and Canonical Matters. Their mandate will be to offer guidance on the question of whether the authority exists for a diocese and a bishop to authorize the blessing same-sex unions upon a resolution of its Synod. I shall be referring a number of specific legal questions to them, and their advice will also be available for study.

These last two new Commissions, on Doctrine and on Canons, will be small in size. I shall appoint people to them with appropriate expertise from across the Anglican Church of Canada, to ensure we have the best national as well as local expertise. In this way we shall demonstrate to the rest of the church that we have no wish to act independently. I shall invite submissions from all interested parties. The work of these Commissions will be available not only to New Westminster but to others who may wish to use it as well.

6. A Rite of Blessing

I shall ask the Bishop's Commission on Liturgy (which already exists) to prepare a rite for the blessing of same-sex unions to be authorized for use in the diocese should the decision be taken in due course to proceed. This is not to pre-judge the outcome of a future vote, but to satisfy the desire to know in advance what such blessings would look like if we were to proceed. The Liturgy Commission will be asked to consult with the Faith and Doctrine Commission to develop a theology for the rite. I will also ask them to draw up guidelines for the admission and pastoral preparation of people seeking the church's blessing on their relationships, and their long-term support afterwards.

Conclusion

These six steps form the basis of my response to Motion 9. I am asking the diocese to continue the study, to continue the dialogue. I am proposing that we move forward slowly, that we move forward together, but that we keep moving. This process will take a full two years. It will require the active participation of every Anglican, of every point of view.

If the Synod of 2001 — or any future Synod — confirms this motion by a clear and substantial majority, and if no substantive legal or canonical impediments are found to exist, I shall be prepared at that time to give my consent to proceed. Until these conditions are met, we shall remain as we are, without prejudice to the fact that either the House of Bishops or the General Synod may wish at some point to take the matter further.

In announcing this decision today, I am deeply conscious that I am asking gay and lesbian Christians, and the many people who stand with them, for continued patience. I am asking you to help us understand more clearly your spiritual vocation within the Body of Christ. I am asking all members of the church to listen to our brothers and sisters in Christ with compassion.

I would ask that no one see this decision as either a victory or a defeat. It is my hope that these measures will further our dialogue rather than end it. I ask each of you to open your hearts to God and to each other. I ask you to enter this period of dialogue cooperatively and not subversively. And I ask your prayers for God's guidance and peace, for me, for our church, and for all who live out their lives in faithfulness with those they love.

+ *Michael Ingham*
Bishop of New Westminster

Source: http://www.vancouver.anglican.ca

SYNOD VOTE TO ASK FOR BLESSINGS OF SAME-SEX UNIONS FALLS SHORT OF MARGIN BISHOP REQUIRES FOR HIS APPROVAL

VANCOUVER. June 2, 2001. — Despite increased support for a motion by the Synod of the Diocese of New Westminster that called for blessing same-sex unions, Bishop Michael Ingham for the second time refused to give his consent to such blessings.

Anglicans — 400 clergy and lay delegates — from 80 parishes in Greater Vancouver, the Fraser Valley, and the Sunshine Coast of British Columbia, voted 226 to 174 to ask the bishop to authorize clergy to bless long-term, "covenanted" homosexual relationships.

"It is clear now that we have a growing acceptance of our gay and lesbian members," Bishop Ingham told the Diocesan Synod after the vote result was announced. But he said the result fell short of the margin he felt necessary for his consent.

"I realize this is a very difficult decision for gay and lesbian people, and I make this decision with some reluctance but with a sense of responsibility both for the unity of this diocese and for collegiality with the wider church to which we belong."

"My decision is in part a pastoral one to those who now find themselves in a minority position — those of traditional conscience who are respected and will be protected in this church and in the diocese."

"We need a little bit more time before the kind of consensus emerges that we will need in order to move forward with a sense of unity," the bishop said.

The vote by the Diocesan Synod, meeting for two days at Capilano College in North Vancouver, followed two and one-half years of study of the issue. After a close vote three years ago — 179 to 170 in favour — the bishop established a lengthy "dialogue process."

Each of the 80 parishes was "twinned" with another. The resulting 40 groups met up to eight times to talk about what the Bible says about homosexuality, what modern theologians say, and what a rite of blessing might look like. Gay and lesbian members of the diocese (and one ex-gay) told the groups what a blessing would mean for them.

When he established the dialogue, Bishop Ingham said he would agree to authorize the blessing of same-sex unions in parishes that wished to do so, if two conditions were met: church lawyers had to advise him he had authority to authorize such blessings, and the Diocesan Synod voted by "a clear and substantial" majority for the motion. Three church lawyers making up a Legal and Canonical Commission so ruled in April that if he so wished he could authorize blessings. The ruling led to today's vote.

"What I think we need to do is sit with the result today for a little while. It's not in my plan to reintroduce Motion 9," he said at a press conference. (Motion 9 was the motion urging the bishop to authorize same-sex blessings.)

The vote followed about three hours of often emotional debate on the floor of well-attended Synod: 400 of 418 lay and clergy delegates eligible came to vote at the Synod, the annual meeting of the Anglican Church in the largest diocese by population in British Columbia.

Proponents argued that it was time gay and lesbian Anglicans were accepted as full members of the church; many said that establishing the blessing was a matter of justice. Opponents argued that the Bible condemned homosexual behaviour, and that blessing same-sex unions would seriously strain the unity of the diocese, and put it out of step with the wider Anglican Church.

Source: http://www.vancouver.anglican.ca

BISHOP MICHAEL INGHAM'S PROPOSAL REGARDING THE BLESSING OF SAME-SEX UNIONS

Presented to the Diocesan Synod, June 14–15, 2002, and accepted by the Synod (as Motion 7)

1. Context

After 25 years of discussion within the Canadian church, our Synod in 1998 and 2001 voted to proceed with the blessing of covenanted same-sex unions. On both occasions, my episcopal consent was withheld. My hope has been to allow time for the development of greater consensus and mutual understanding.

In the 12 months since Synod 2001 it appears the issue remains contentious and far from resolution. Gay and lesbian members of our church feel their pastoral needs are being denied despite majority support from Synods. Other Anglicans express sincere commitment to the church but feel they would be pastorally isolated if I were to give my consent in the future.

2. A Proposal

In order to resolve the impasse, and to enable the highest level of communion to continue within the diocese, I offer the following proposal as a way forward.

A. Appointment of Episcopal Visitor

I will appoint a Canadian bishop from outside this diocese to offer pastoral care to those parishes and clergy who desire it. It is to be understood that this is a temporary measure, renewable annually by vestry vote and with my consent, while the diocese and the affected parishes continue to work toward mutual reconciliation.

The Diocesan Bishop shall retain canonical authority over all parishes and licensed clergy, including jurisdiction in all episcopal acts, while delegating pastoral oversight to the Visitor. The Visitor shall be accountable to the Diocesan. Costs shall be borne by the diocese for an initial period of three years, renewable. Parishes under the care of the Episcopal Visitor shall continue to meet their financial obligations to the diocese.

B. Conscience Clause

No member of the diocese, lay or ordained, shall be required to act against their conscience in the blessing of same-sex unions. There shall be no discrimination against any member of the diocese in respect of employment, appointment or advancement on grounds of conscience. No "sunset clause" is intended, although I cannot bind my successors in this matter.

Clergy holding or seeking the bishop's license must honour the conscience of others (as on other matters such as the ordination of women), maintain collegiality including attendance at clergy events, and respect the decisions of Synod. The Bishop's Expectations of Clergy, published in the Diocesan Procedures Manual, shall continue to apply to all diocesan clergy. Failure to comply may result in the termination of license.

C. Rite of Blessing

I shall approve a rite of blessing, subject to review by the Legal and Canonical Commission. Requests to use the rite must be made in writing indicating the consent of both the Incumbent and the congregation, by vestry vote. Only those parishes meeting these conditions shall be authorised to offer such pastoral services.

Source: http://www.vancouver.anglican.ca

STATEMENT BY THE BISHOP OF NEW WESTMINSTER FOLLOWING THE ANNOUNCEMENT OF THE RESULT OF THE VOTE ON THE BLESSING OF SAME-SEX UNIONS

June 15, 2002

The Synod of the Diocese of New Westminster has now made a clear decision about the pastoral care of Anglicans in this part of Canada.

We have voted not to compel but to permit: to permit those parishes that wish to celebrate permanent, intimate, loving relationships between persons of the same sex to do so in recognition of the God-given goodness of their sacred mutual commitments; and to permit those parishes who stand in continuity with the historic practice of the church, and with biblical truth as they sincerely believe it, to do so without compulsion, with full protection of conscience, and with the pastoral support of episcopal ministry.

We take these steps today in full awareness that others in the Anglican Communion may not understand our actions. We hope all will realize that Canadian Anglicans live in a country where homosexual activity was decriminalized thirty years ago; where human rights legislation offers legal protection to gay and lesbian people against all forms of discrimination; and where churches across this great country freely and openly welcome men and women of every language, race and nation, colour, marital status and sexual orientation. We are an inclusive church in a plural, peaceful and tolerant society.

We are not compromising the Christian faith nor relativising its moral teaching. We are extending to gay and lesbian Christians the same freedom that is enjoyed by others to commit their lives to Jesus Christ together, and the same obligation to grow in the costly demands of love. We are calling them to fidelity, permanence and stability in relationships. We are offering them the support of the Christian community as they grow into the fullness of the stature of Christ through the struggles and challenges of mutual commitment.

No one is being excluded from our fellowship today. We have not taken sides with one group in our church against another. We have chosen to live together in mutual respect. We acknowledge and repent of the pain we have caused in the course of this long process. We are deeply aware that there is much more work to do to build up mutual understanding and reconciliation. In this we ask for the support of the wider church, not condemnation, and patience from those who live in very different social contexts from our own.

We have voted for unity in the midst of diversity. We have decided to embrace faithful Christian believers of differing conscience within the one Body of Christ. We are not taking sides with some members of our church over against others, but inviting both to work together to support the mission of the church throughout the world without the scandal of division.

We do these things in the belief that they are the call of the Spirit to the church everywhere. To the Spirit of God and to the church we pledge our continued loyalty and affection.

Source: http://www.vancouver.anglican.ca

APPENDIX I
The BC Referendum on Treaty Negotiations

[The following is the text of a brochure on the topic of the referendum distributed by the Government of British Columbia]

Your Guide to the Referendum

> "We are committed to negotiating workable, affordable treaty settlements that will provide certainty, finality and equality.
>
> Treaties offer the promise of a New Era of hope, economic opportunity and greater self-determination for all aboriginal people. But, for too long, most British Columbians have felt shut out of the process."
> — A New Era for British Columbia, 2001

The referendum on principles for treaty negotiations is an opportunity for you to have a direct say on an issue of vital importance to us all.

It's an opportunity for you to help determine the principles that should guide our Province's approach to treaty negotiations.

It will provide certainty for our Province's negotiating position. It will help reinvigorate the treaty process.

And it will build a foundation for a new relationship with First Nations that ensures aboriginal British Columbians share fully in a prosperous future.

In the nine years since the treaty process was established by the province, federal government and First Nations, almost half-a-billion dollars has been spent on negotiations — and not one settlement has been achieved. That's created frustration and uncertainty for all of us, aboriginal and non-aboriginal alike.

We believe it's time you had the opportunity to be included in this process. Our Government committed to giving you a say on BC's principles for treaty negotiations. And it's a commitment that British Columbians entrusted us to honour.

The principles we're asking you to consider address basic issues important to all of us — issues involving land use, resources, taxation and how we are governed; issues on which all British Columbians deserve to have their views heard.

Our government is committed to negotiating workable, affordable settlements that provide certainty, finality and equality. That commitment is not up for debate.

This is not a referendum on minority rights. As the BC Supreme Court has made clear, it is not possible for this referendum to violate those rights. Aboriginal rights and title are protected under our Constitution. Those rights are not up for debate.

This is an opportunity for all of us to understand our constitutional obligations to aboriginal people, and to discuss how we can move forward with settlements in a way that has public trust and confidence — to help fast-track treaty negotiations and forge a new relationship with First Nations.

I invite you to read this brochure, to discuss and consider the issues, and to make your vote count.

Together, we can revitalize negotiations and build a future that harmonizes the needs of all British Columbians — aboriginal and non-aboriginal alike.

Honourable Gordon Campbell, Premier of British Columbia

The Principles

The following eight principles are being considered to guide the Province's approach to treaty negotiations. Do you agree?

Whereas the Government of British Columbia is committed to negotiating workable, affordable treaty settlements that will provide certainty, finality and equality;

1. Do you agree that the Provincial Government should adopt the principle that private property should not be expropriated for treaty settlements?

Explanation

This principle asks voters to confirm that Government should not use its legislative powers to take private property to transfer to First Nations in treaty settlements.

Government's Perspective

Treaties are about the settlement of land claims; treaty negotiations are about rights in land. Approval of this principle means Government would use crown land for treaty settlement and would not expropriate private lands without permission. A yes vote would not prevent owners of land from selling their land for inclusion in treaties on a willing seller and willing buyer basis.

By law Government can expropriate lands to meet a public interest, such as highways. This principle would provide additional protection against expropriation of private property to ensure that private property is not expropriated for use in treaties.

A no vote would maintain the current law that allows Government to negotiate treaties with the same approach it takes to building highways — by expropriating land for treaty settlement where necessary in the public interest.

2. Do you agree that the Provincial Government should adopt the principle that the terms and conditions of leases and licences should be respected; and fair compensation for unavoidable disruption of commercial interests should be ensured?

Explanation

The Province should negotiate treaty settlements that respect the terms and conditions of leases and licences previously issued by the Crown. Fair compensation should be paid if the lease or licence is adversely affected.

Government's Perspective

It is the goal of Government to minimize the impacts of treaties on leases and licences on Crown land. This principle is not about private property, but Crown land that people and companies have the right to use for specific needs. These tenures are a basis of key commercial activity — forestry, mining, ecotourism — and large investments have been made in these sectors of the economy. Examples include forestry licences, grazing leases, and recreational leases.

Government supports a principle that respects these tenures. This principle also ensures that, if impacts are unavoidable, compensation for the disruption will be paid. This would expand the current approach to compensation to include all commercial interests adversely affected by treaty negotiations, whether or not there is a legal obligation.

As compensation is a cost to Government, negotiators will be strongly motivated to respect existing leases and licences.

A no to this principle would mean that, although impacts on leases and licences would be kept to a minimum, Government would not be obliged to compensate for all impacts.

3. Do you agree that the Provincial Government should adopt the principle that hunting, fishing and recreational opportunities on Crown land should be ensured for all British Columbians?

Explanation

British Columbians, subject to federal and provincial laws, should be able to go onto Crown land for hunting, fishing and recreational purposes, as they have in the past.

Government's Perspective

At each negotiating table, issues of land and resource management — both on First Nations lands and on Crown land are common themes. As treaties move towards defining aboriginal rights to hunting, fishing and other traditional pursuits, so too should Government protect non-aboriginal access to land for these activities.

Many British Columbians use Crown land for fishing, hunting, and recreation. Approval of this principle would direct negotiators to negotiate terms in treaties that ensure that, outside lands transferred to First Nations for treaty settlement, these activities will continue. This would mean the Government would not support exclusive access to these opportunities on Crown land by First Nations as a result of treaties.

A no vote would indicate that BC need not demand that this be so, and those opportunities may be affected.

4. Do you agree that the Provincial Government should adopt the principle that parks and protected areas should be maintained for the use and benefit of all British Columbians?

Explanation

The Province should negotiate settlements that maintain the integrity of British Columbia's system of parks and protected areas and ensure that all British Columbians will continue to benefit from the recreational opportunities offered by these areas.

Government's Perspective

First Nations have asserted title over different lands in British Columbia, including parks and protected areas. It is clear to Government that all parties, First Nations included, have a strong commitment to the values that protect the unique spaces of BC.

Support of this principle would instruct government negotiators to work to ensure that a system of parks and protected areas will remain available for the use and benefit of all British Columbians.

A no vote would mean that provincial negotiators need not be guided by this principle when issues concerning parks and protected areas are raised in negotiations.

5. Do you agree that the Provincial Government should adopt the principle that province-wide standards of resource management and environmental protection should continue to apply?

Explanation

Activities on treaty settlement land that involve the use of or affect natural resources or the environment will be subject to control. These activities should at least meet the minimum standards of resource management and environmental protection that apply across the province.

Government's Perspective

Managing resources for the good of all British Columbians is a fundamental obligation of Government. Support of this principle would direct the province's negotiators to insist that treaties result in environmental protection and resource management standards that meet or beat provincial standards. These would be minimum standards, and First Nations would be free to implement higher standards for their lands if they chose.

A no vote would mean there would be no need at the table to insist on the use of provincial minimum standards on treaty settlement land.

6. Do you agree that the Provincial Government should adopt the principle that aboriginal self-government should have the characteristics of local government, with powers delegated from Canada and British Columbia?

Explanation

This principle relates to the Province's position that the powers of a First Nation's government should be delegated from either the Parliament of Canada or the Legislature of British Columbia, instead of being based on an inherent right to self-government

Government's Perspective

Some measure of self-government currently exists through the Indian Act, but it is a flawed self-government model that does not support the needs of aboriginal people.

BC supports self-government for aboriginal people. The question this principle asks is what model or type of self-government BC supports in treaties.

The Government has been clear about the model it supports. It is a tested model, with examples in Sechelt and Yukon land claims agreements. It is a model where the First Nation government has the characteristics of local government, with powers delegated from the Legislative Assembly of BC and Parliament of Canada. And it is a model that is democratically accountable to the people under its jurisdiction (including non-aboriginal people). A yes vote will be a clear mandate to uphold our stated position.

A no vote would mean BC would not be restricted to this model when negotiating; other models that have been discussed could be supported. Examples of other models include those where First Nation self-government powers are paramount to the powers of BC and Canada. A no vote would mean BC would negotiate self-government, but the options and number of potential models would be broader and less certain.

7. Do you agree that the Provincial Government should adopt the principle that treaties should include mechanisms for harmonizing land use planning between aboriginal governments and neighbouring local governments?

Explanation

Treaty provisions would encourage aboriginal governments and local governments to collaborate on local land use planning and development issues, and to assist in resolving any disagreements.

Government's Perspective

Treaties will include the ability of First Nations governments to plan and control lands under their jurisdiction or authority. Many First Nations and neighbouring local governments are already working to establish effective relationships. This principle seeks to build on these successes by ensuring this goal is pursued at treaty tables.

We believe that BC should encourage tools that will ensure coordination of land use planning between aboriginal governments and neighbouring local governments for the good of both communities. Approval of this principle will not give a veto to local government on what happens on First Nations land or vice versa.

A no vote would mean BC's negotiators need not insist upon negotiating such provisions.

8. Do you agree that the Provincial Government should adopt the principle that the existing tax exemptions for aboriginal people should be phased out?

Explanation

This principle refers to the tax exemptions that presently exist in the Indian Act, which states that some kinds of personal property and employment income are not taxable. The term "phased out" refers to a gradual change from that kind of tax exemption to full tax equality.

Government's Perspective

Approval of this principle to phase out exemptions over a fair period would provide more aboriginal people an opportunity to help support the activities of all governments, including their own. It would mean that BC supports tax equality.

A no vote would mean the provincial voice on this issue would not need to be heard.

"The Government takes a position on these questions. We would answer yes to each of them. Answering yes to these questions will provide the province's negotiators with a clear mandate on issues that have arisen and will continue to arise in the course of negotiations."

Honourable Geoff Plant, Attorney General and Minister Responsible for Treaty Negotiations

APPENDIX J
The Response of the Anglican Church in British Columbia to the Referendum on Treaty Negotiations

THE ANGLICAN PROVINCIAL SYNOD OF BRITISH COLUMBIA AND YUKON

The Most Rev. David Crawley
Archbishop and Metropolitan

PRESS RELEASE

Bishops to tell Anglicans throughout British Columbia Treaty Negotiations Referendum raises "serious questions"

All four Anglican bishops in British Columbia are telling church members throughout British Columbia that the provincial referendum on Aboriginal treaty negotiations raises "serious questions."

In a pastoral letter to be read from pulpits all across the province next Sunday, the bishops refer all Anglicans to the recommendations of an Anglican Task Force that urges a "no" vote, or a protest vote.

The bishops, spiritual leaders to Anglicans in about 200 churches and congregations in the province, say that the decision how to vote is "a matter of individual conscience." But they urge church members "to study and learn about the complexities of treaty claims and negotiations" and emphasize the Anglican Task Force's recommendations.

The 18-member Task Force recommended to Anglicans that if they choose to participate in the referendum, they should vote "no" to all questions. If they choose not to participate, they should register a protest rather than spoil their ballots.

The provincial government started conducting the provincial Aboriginal Treaty Negotiations Referendum this week by sending out mail-in ballots, which are due back May 15. The referendum consists of eight questions, each to be answered "yes" or "no."

The Most Rev. David Crawley, Archbishop of Kootenay and the chief bishop (or "Metropolitan") in British Columbia, in the pastoral letter signed by all four bishops, says that Anglicans come before God "as the same, penitent sinners … no one gets more, no one gets less." In view of what he calls this "radical equality," Crawley questions the very idea of a referendum on Aboriginal treaties.

"Should or indeed can the rights of a minority, which have been acknowledged to exist by the courts of the land, be subject of a vote by a majority?" asks Crawley in the pastoral letter.

The pastoral letter also asks how the government could consider a referendum to be binding "no matter how few citizens take part in it," and questions whether the referendum will enhance or harm the treaty process.

Much care should be given to the decision on how or whether to participate in the referendum, the letter says. adding that the bishops believe that for the next decade the relationship between First Nations peoples and non-Aboriginal peoples is likely to be "the dominant political, social, economic, and justice issue" in the province.

Joining in the statement with Crawley are Bishops Barry Jenks of the Diocese of British Columbia (which covers Vancouver island), Michael Ingham of the Diocese of New Westminster (which covers the Lower Mainland), and William Anderson of the Diocese of Caledonia (Northern BC). Crawley himself has charge of the Diocese of Kootenay plus the Churches of the Central Interior of the province.

The Task Force was made up of both priests and lay members, and reported to Crawley last week. It included Anglicans from all areas of the province, both Aboriginal and non-Aboriginal. It was chaired by Chief Alfred Scow, OC, a retired provincial court judge and hereditary Kwicksutaineuk chief, and a member of Christ Church Cathedral in Vancouver.

For further information, please contact:

CRAIG VANCE, diocesan Church and Society consultant
604 684-6306; 604 730-8326
NEALE ADAMS, diocesan Communications Officer
604 684-6306, ext. 23; 604 873-0568; 604 928-8784 (cellular)

Source: http://www.vancouver.anglican.ca

BC BISHOPS' PASTORAL LETTER ON THE REFERENDUM

Dear Sisters and Brothers in Christ,

We, the Bishops of British Columbia, write to you on a matter that concerns all Christians and citizens of this province. At the very core of our faith lies the concept of "radical equality." When we come to the altar to receive the Body and Blood of our Lord, we all come as the same, penitent sinners, and we all receive the same gift of grace. No one gets more; no one gets less. True Christian community is based not on common interests, social standing or life circumstances, but on making real among us this "radical equality." The extent to which we do so is the extent to which we reflect the Realm of God. Further, as individual Christians and as communities of Christians, our purpose is to bring the Realm of God into being in our world. We do so by struggling to extend throughout society the "radical equality" that is the nature of the Realm of God.

As citizens of British Columbia, we are asked to take part in what is being called a Referendum on Treaty Negotiations. Some months ago, a Task Force to study the issue was set up jointly by the Diocese of New Westminster and Archbishop Crawley, the Metropolitan. The Task Force is broadly based geographically and includes aboriginal Christians.

The "referendum" raises serious questions for us.

1. Should or indeed can the rights of a minority, which have been acknowledged to exist by the courts of the land, be the subject of a vote by the majority?

2. Is this a true referendum or is it more accurately described as a poll? Is it right for the government to consider the results of such a ballot binding no matter how few citizens take part in it?

3. Will the "referendum" enhance or harm the process of treaty negotiations which are necessary for the "common good" of our province?

4. How should we, as Christians, respond to the "referendum ballot" when we receive it?

The answer to the last question is, of course, a matter of individual conscience. The Task Force recommends the following:

a. If you choose to participate in the balloting, vote no to all questions.

b. If, because you disapprove of the very idea of the referendum, you choose not to participate, do not destroy your ballot. Instead, sign the certification envelope as a registered voter but leave the ballot blank and mail it in as instructed. Your ballot will be recorded and reported as a rejected ballot.

Finally, we ask all Anglicans to study and learn about the complexities of treaty claims and negotiations. There will be articles in various diocesan papers and a number already have been posted on the web site of the Diocese of New Westminster.

We believe the dominant political, social, economic and justice issue in the life of British Columbia for the next ten years will be the relationship of aboriginal and non-aboriginal peoples and cultures.

To this end, we invite all members of the church to consider the gravity of the choices before us in the light of our vocation to bring into reality the Realm of God.

Yours in Christ,

David Crawley, Archbishop of Kootenay
Metropolitan of British Columbia and Yukon
Bishop for the Central Interior
Barry Jenks, Bishop of British Columbia
Michael Ingham, Bishop of New Westminster
William Anderson, Bishop of Caledonia

Source: http://www.vancouver.anglican.ca

APPENDIX K
The Result of the British Columbia Referendum on Treaty Negotiations

Elections BC mailed out a little over 2.1 million Treaty Negotiations Referendum ballots to registered British Columbian voters. Not counting discarded ballots that were not returned properly, 763,480 ballots, representing 35.83 per cent of registered voters, were returned. This participation rate is only half of the 71 per cent voter turnout at the May 2001 BC provincial government election.

The referendum was an eight-part plebiscite. For each question, around 7.5 per cent of the votes were rejected as invalidly cast. Considering only the valid votes, all eight questions received very large majorities of yes votes, with no question getting less than 84 per cent yes votes, and only questions one and six getting less than 90 per cent yes votes.

Full results of the vote are available online at:
http://www.elections.bc.ca/referendum/finalresults.pdf

The BC government was pleased with the results. Premier Gordon Campbell said that the results "mark a crucial milestone in the long march towards treaty-making in British Columbia," and that the voters had "given their provincial government a clear mandate and a solid set of principles to get on with the task" of negotiating "workable, affordable treaties that will provide certainty, finality and equality."

The full text of the Premier's remarks is online at:
http://os8150.pb.gov.bc.ca/4dcgi/nritem?5462

First Nations groups were dismissive of the results, pointing out that since over 1.5 million voters either did not vote or voted no, only a minority of BC voters had endorsed the government's position.

Chief Stewart Philip, president of the Union of British Columbia Indian Chiefs, said that pollsters had criticized the referendum's questions as one-sided and designed to generate votes biased in favor of the government's position. He warned that the referendum's results might "create unacceptable pre-conditions to future treaty negotiations," and might "prove to be a 'mill stone' as opposed to the 'milestone' proclaimed by Premier Campbell," further bogging down the treaty process.

Press release at:
http://www.ubcic.bc.ca/docs/UBCICPress_referendum_070402.pdf

The First Nations Summit provides support to First Nations tribes in their treaty negotiations with the government. In a press release, the FNS called the referendum "a stalling tactic" designed to impose the BC government's "limited views at treaty tables." FNS member Lydia Hwitsum called the referendum "a reason for a year being wasted at the negotiation table," and expressed hope that "effective good faith treaty negotiations" could now resume.

Press release at:
http://www.fns.bc.ca/pdf/Referendum_July2002.pdf

ABC Publishing
ANGLICAN BOOK CENTRE

All Who Minister
New Ways of Serving God's People
Maylanne Maybee, editor
These first-hand stories from the frontiers of alternative ministry, and ground-breaking articles on the theology of ministry, offer inspiring models and rationales for all who minister — whether in a venerable tradition or on the forefront of change. Exciting and creative!
1-55126-341-6 $24.95

Seeking the Seekers
Serving the Hidden Spiritual Quest
Paul MacLean and Michael Thompson
Using an approach that congregations can readily follow, the authors develop practical and effective strategies to reconnect with people's daily lives and inject new relevance into the church's mission.
1-55126-308-4 $16.95

Alive Again
Recession and Recovery in the Churches
Reginald Stackhouse
In this fascinating study of "growth churches" across Canada, Stackhouse recounts real stories about real churches he has visited and considers the reasons for their exceptional growth.
1-55126-257-6 $16.95

Mourners and Midwives
Choices for the 21st-Century Church
Herbert O'Driscoll
A richly illustrated look at human accomplishment — a scientific , artistic, social, and spiritual perspective — that encourages us to envision a realistic and vibrant future of Christianity and the church. Three-part video with study manual.
1-55126-231-2 $99.95

Longing for God
Primate's Theological Commission
Anglican Church of Canada
How do we interpret God's word to us? How does it shape the way we live? Our understanding of the Bible deeply influences how we think and feel, how we live and work with others. It affects every aspect of our lives, personally and globally.
1-55126-343-2 $18.95

Turning to God
Primate's Theological Commission
Anglican Church of Canada
Can we be fully human and truly Christian at the same time? In this resource, the authors delve deeply into issues of Christian living, and grapple with questions about prayer, the sacraments, conversion, discipleship, and Native spirituality.
1-55126-344-0 $18.95

Anglican Diversity
Challenges for the 21st Century
Patricia Bays
A knowledgeable and sympathetic look at the Anglican Church today, showing how diversity is its strength.
1-55126-327-0 $14.95